Acclaim for HENRY

CORNEL WEST's

The Future of the Race

"Consistently thoughtful and often poignant. . . . Gates writes intimately and affectionately. . . . West masterfully interweaves . . . history with developments in literature and the arts. . . . Each shows us that human progress will not be denied." —*Boston Sunday Globe*

"Gates is engagingly witty and journalistic. . . . West grasps for prophecy . . . performing something of an intellectual tour de force." —*The New York Times Book Review*

"An important volume . . . thoughtful and deeply felt . . . a useful introduction to . . . the question that has plagued African American intellectuals for over 200 years." —*Kirkus Reviews*

"A striking departure . . . stunning." —*Washington Times*

"A refreshing way to think about race in the United States today." —*Christian Science Monitor*

"Raises important and stimulating questions. . . . Learned, brilliant and provocative . . . Henry Louis Gates and Cornel West consort atop the apex of American intellectual life." —*Portland Oregonian*

D0034255

HENRY LOUIS GATES, JR.
CORNEL WEST

The Future of the Race

Henry Louis Gates, Jr., was born and raised in Mineral County, West Virginia. He graduated phi beta kappa and summa cum laude from Yale College with a degree in history and was a London correspondent for *Time* magazine before receiving his Ph.D. in English from Cambridge University. He writes frequently for such publications as *The New York Times Book Review, The New Yorker,* and *The New Republic*; his books include *Colored People* (which won several national awards), *Figures in Black, The Signifying Monkey* (for which he received an American Book Award), and *Loose Canons.* He is now W. E. B. Du Bois Professor of the Humanities and chair of the Department of Afro-American Studies at Harvard University.

Cornel West was born in Tulsa, Oklahoma, and grew up in Sacramento, California. He graduated magna cum laude in three years from Harvard College and received his Ph.D. from Princeton University, where he was Professor of Religion and Director of Afro-American Studies. He is now Professor of Afro-American Studies and of the Philosophy of Religion at Harvard University, and has been a guest lecturer at many campuses. His eleven books include *Race Matters, Keeping Faith, Prophetic Fragments, The American Evasion of Philosophy,* and, with bell hooks, *Breaking Bread: Insurgent Black Intellectual Life.*

THE FUTURE OF THE RACE

THE FUTURE OF THE RACE

by HENRY LOUIS GATES, JR.

and CORNEL WEST

Vintage Books

A DIVISION OF RANDOM HOUSE, INC.

NEW YORK

FIRST VINTAGE BOOKS EDITION, JANUARY 1997

Copyright © 1996 by Henry Louis Gates, Jr., and Cornel West

All rights reserved under International and Pan-American Copyright
Conventions. Published in the United States by Vintage Books,
a division of Random House, Inc., New York, and simultaneously in
Canada by Random House of Canada Limited, Toronto. Originally
published in hardcover by Alfred A. Knopf, Inc.,
New York, in 1996.

Library of Congress Cataloging-in-Publication Data:
Gates, Henry Louis.
The future of the race / by Henry Louis Gates, Jr. and Cornel West.
p. cm.
Originally published: New York : A.A. Knopf, 1996.
Includes bibliographical references.
ISBN 0-679-76378-3
1. Afro-Americans—Social conditions—1975–
2. Afro-American leadership. 3. Afro-American intellectuals.
4. Upper classes—United States. 5. United States—Race relations.
I. West, Cornel. II. Title.
E185.86.G377 1997
305.8'00973—dc20 96-28273
CIP

Random House Web address: http://www.randomhouse.com/

Printed in the United States of America
20 19 18 17 16 15 14 13 12

Contents

PREFACE

THIS BOOK resulted from a series of conversations in which we have been engaged over the past two years, at the offices of the Department of Afro-American Studies at Harvard University, where we are both professors charged with the task of building a premier research and teaching program in African-American Studies. In the corridor of the department sits a bronze bust of W. E. B. Du Bois. Du Bois was a member of the Harvard College Class of 1890, and then he earned a Ph.D. in history at Harvard in 1895. In 1903, he published an essay entitled "The Talented Tenth," which sought to define the commitment to service that the black college graduate owes to the rest of the black community.

We and our colleagues regularly engage in discussions about the nature and function of our department—as well as its responsibilities (ours, as professors, and those of our students) to the larger African-American community, past, present, and future. A central part of our mission as teachers is to analyze, and reinterpret for our generation, the great writings of the black past, showing how they continue to speak to us today. Just as the English literary critic F. R. Leavis regularly undertook what he called "revaluations" of canonical works in the pages of his journal, *Scrutiny,* so too do we think it incumbent upon our generation of scholars to ground our understanding of the present in the germinal thought of our collective past.

One such effort has produced this book, in which we, two "grandchildren" of the group of intellectuals Du Bois dubbed "the Talented Tenth," have sought to think through—and critique—Du Bois's challenge of commitment to service that, we deeply believe, the formally educated owe to all those who have not benefited from the expanded opportunities afforded by the gains in civil rights and its concomitant, the programmatic attempt to fulfill America's commitment to equal opportunity, popularly known as "affirmative action."

This is not intended to be a book that makes policy recommendations, although we both have strong feelings about the need for both governmental and private forms of intervention to reverse the delimitation of life choices that all too many African Americans face. Rather, this is a book of reflection, consisting of two essays that map our separate responses to Du Bois's provocative thesis.

For Gates, this response takes the form of an autobiographical account of the triumph and tragedies of the generation of young blacks who attended historically white institutions, such as Yale University, where he was an undergraduate in the late sixties and early seventies. Within this frame, he explores today's paradox of the largest black middle class in American history coexisting with one of the largest black underclasses.

West's essay investigates the nature of Du Bois's life and thought and the tensions inherent between them. West analyzes Du Bois as a thinker, focusing particularly on his political and philosophical ideas. He explicates Du Bois's thought by situating him in the context of his times and within the limitations imposed by his social, political, and intellectual milieu. Using this framework, he then meditates upon "black strivings" (as Du Bois put it) as we face the end of the American century.

In *The Future of the Race,* we explore a pivotal aspect of Du Bois's intellectual legacy, and so have included the essay to which we are responding, as well as Du Bois's own critique of it (first published in 1948, and reprinted here in its entirety for the first time). For those readers who are unfamiliar with either text, we have also provided a historical overview of Du Bois's life and works, to serve as an introduction to his two essays found in our Appendix.

Twenty-five years ago, historically white male institutions of higher learning—such as Yale and Harvard—opened their doors to blacks and women in unprecedented numbers, a direct result of so-called "affirmative action" lobbying for the diversification of America's middle classes. Harvard and Yale, where we were undergraduates, were both quite self-conscious about their new admissions policies. At Yale, for example, Kingman Brewster, addressing the entering class in September of 1969 in a speech crafted more for the benefit of the "old Blue" alumni and the press than of those students seated in Woolsey Hall, welcomed each as one of that year's "1,000 male leaders." Pointing rather awkwardly to the "250 women" sitting in the audience, he promised that, despite their presence, Yale would never abandon its commitment to what at the turn of the century Du Bois had called America's "exceptional men."

If Yale went coed in 1969, never before had it seen more color in its classes: of the Class of 1973, ninety-six students, or 7.9 percent, were black, compared with eighteen students, or 1.8 percent, of the Class of 1968. Often "first-generation Ivy," and sometimes first-generation college, these students congregated in the pre-med and pre-law curricula, in search of security in the soon-to-be-integrated professional circles, especially the law, medicine, journalism, and business. But while they sought to enter the traditional professions—the academy, curiously enough, was not a popular option—a remarkably large percentage sought knowledge about their cultural and their ethnic heritages in the newly established programs in Afro-American Studies.

It is one of the dramatic—and, we believe, defining—facts of our generation that the birth of Afro-American Studies and the influx of a "critical" number of black students coincided on the campuses of America's historically white research colleges and universities. The agitation of black students, of course, had led to the creation of African-American Studies as an academic field in 1969, both at Harvard and Yale and throughout the country. Many of us took at least one Afro-American Studies course per term, as much to bolster the enrollment of these fledgling programs as to help retrace an invisible scaffolding that we felt undergirded us as citizens and as intellectuals. We were seeking to read and understand the canonical texts of the black tradition, which, we hoped, would enable us to tap into a vast black cultural "unconscious."

No less than three times that year—the year that culminated in strikes all across America's college campuses, called to protest the Viet Nam War—Gates was a student in classes assigned to read Harold Cruse's *The Crisis of the Negro Intellectual* and Du Bois's "The Talented Tenth." These were the two signal works in the black tradition meant to help us find our way through the abyss of integration.

"The Talented Tenth" was held up as a model for the social, political, and ethical role of the members of what we might call a "crossover" generation, those of us who, as a result of the great civil rights movement, were able to integrate historically white educational and professional institutions. Cornel West and Henry Louis Gates, Jr., in other words, were trained at Harvard and Yale, respectively, only as a result of the pressure of affirmative action to end these schools' racist quotas, which had barely been disturbed for over a century. (Harvard graduated its first black American only in 1870, 234 years after it was founded.) Had it not been for affirmative action, we, like so many of our ancestors, familial and fraternal, would have met at one of the superb historically black colleges or universities, such as Spelman or Talladega, Howard or Morehouse, Fisk or Lincoln, and not in the Ivy League. It is no accident that 25 years later, we are colleagues on the faculty of one of these very institutions.

More than a quarter of a century later, since that dreadful day in 1968 when Dr. King was so brutally murdered, the size of the black middle class—again, primarily because of affirmative action—has quadrupled, doubling in the 1980s alone. Simultaneously—

and paradoxically—the size of the black underclass has grown disproportionately as well: in 1995, 45 percent of all black children are born at, or beneath, the poverty line. Economists have shown that fully one-third of the members of the African-American community are *worse off* economically today than they were the day that King was killed. *If it is the best of times for the black middle class—the heirs of Du Bois's "Talented Tenth"—it is the worst of times for an equally large segment of our community.*

That American society has failed to protect the basic, ostensibly inalienable rights of its people—equal access to education, adequate housing, affordable medical care, and equal economic opportunity—equal access, indeed, to hope itself—and that the leadership of the African-American community has a special responsibility to attend to these rights, to analyze the peculiar compounding effect of race, gender, and class, and to design, promote, lobby, and agitate for bold and imaginative remedies to conditions of inequality and injustice—these are the underlying premises of this book. We decided to begin to address these complex issues by rereading the essay that sought to define the "ethical content" of our "ethnic identities," as Cornel West has put it—the moral responsibilities of black leadership.

Precisely now, so near to the turn of the century, when the right wing of the Republican Party and a slim majority of the Supreme Court would seem to be hell-bent on dismantling the very legal principles that led to the integration of women and people of color into the larger American middle class to an unprecedented degree—programs that indirectly result in the presence of a black person such as Mr. Justice Clarence Thomas on that very Court, for example—and when pseudoscientific arguments such as those put forth in Charles Murray and Richard J. Herrnstein's *The Bell Curve* seek to use the sanction of "scientific" or "objective" inquiry to justify the dissolution of compensatory education and entitlement programs, we both feel that it is urgent to make this argument now, to generate even deeper reflection on the nature of the society in which we live, the sort of country that we want to inhabit, and want our children's children to inhabit, in the century to come. And we would like to contribute in our small way to the creation of innovative policies that we hope will emerge from discussions such as these.

Race differences and class differentials have been ground together in this country in a crucible of misery and squalor, in such a way that few of us know where one stops and the other begins. But we do know that the causes of poverty within the black community are both *structural* and *behavioral,* as the sociological studies of William J. Wilson have amply demonstrated, and we would be foolish to deny this. A household in which its occupants cannot sustain themselves economically cannot possibly harbor hope or optimism, or stimulate eager participation in the full prerogatives of citizenship. One of our tasks, it seems to us, is to lobby for those social programs that have made a demonstrable difference in the lives of those sufficiently motivated to seize these expanded opportunities, and to reinforce those programs that reignite motivation in the face of despair.

More important, however, we have to demand a structural change in this country, the equivalent of a Marshall Plan for our cities, as the National Urban League has called for repeatedly. We have to take people off welfare, train them for occupations relevant to the highly technological economy of the twenty-first century, and put them to work. Joblessness, as Wilson has shown, is the central cause of our country's so-called racial crisis. The figure in the carpet of America's racial crisis, we are arguing, is economic scarcity and unequal opportunity.

And while we favor a wide array of economic incentives to generate new investment in inner cities, youth apprenticeships with corporations, expanded tax credits for earned income, and tenant ownership of inner-city property, we believe that we must face the reality that economic prosperity and corporate investment will not come easily to our inner cities and we should most probably begin to think about moving black inner-city workers to sites where new jobs are being created, rather than merely holding our breath waiting for new factories or industries to crop up miraculously in the inner city.

That said, we strongly support Urban League President Hugh Price's proposals to develop the economic health of black neighborhoods in America's cities:

Promoting economic development means that all of our children must understand and become comfortable with entrepreneurship. Too many of them have an unrealistic sense of the way things work or just don't know what their possibilities are. We must help them understand that they can earn a decent and honorable living through operating very small businesses. . . .

Many cities are experiencing economic revivals. They are doing so by emphasizing what I call "quality of life" industries. They are building stadiums, museums and aquariums downtown. They are restoring downtown restaurant, entertainment and residential districts. Some are even building unsubsidized single-family housing within walking distance of downtown. Our entrepreneurs should be in the middle of all that action. We need investment banks to assure access to capital for these enterprises. That is why the idea of an investment trust that the Leadership Summit is developing is intriguing.[1]

It is only by confronting the twin realities of white racism, on the one hand, and our own failures to seize initiative and break the cycle of poverty, on the other, that we, the remnants of the Talented Tenth, will be able to assume a renewed leadership role for, and within, the black community. We must stand boldly against *any* manifestation of antiblack racism, whatever form it might take. On this matter, there can be *no* compromise. But to continue to repeat the same old stale formulas, to blame "the man" for oppressing us all, in exactly the same ways; to scapegoat Koreans, Jews, women, or even black immigrants for the failure of African Americans to seize local entrepreneurial opportunities, is to neglect our duty as leaders of our own community.

Not to demand that each member of the black community accept individual responsibility for her or his behavior—whether that behavior assumes the form of black-on-black homicide, violations by gang members against the sanctity of the church, unprotected sexual activity, gangster rap lyrics, misogyny and homophobia—is to function merely as ethnic cheerleaders selling woof tickets from the campus or the suburbs, rather than saying the difficult things that may be unpopular with our fellows. Being a leader does not necessarily mean being loved; loving one's community means daring to risk estrangement and alienation from that very community, in the short run, in order to break the cycle of poverty, despair, and hopelessness that we are in, over the long run. For what is at stake is nothing less than the survival of our country, *and* the African-American people.

Just as we must continue to fight so that more people of color are admitted to the student bodies and hired on the faculty and staff of our colleges and universities, and integrated into every phase of America's social and commercial life, we must fight to see that Congress and the President enact a comprehensive jobs bill. And finally, to help bridge the painful gap between those of us on campus and those of us left behind on the streets, we call upon the African-American Studies departments in this country to institutionalize sophomore and junior year summer internships for public service and community development, in cooperation with organizations such as the black church, the Children's Defense Fund, the National Urban League, the NAACP, PUSH, etc., so that we can begin to combat teenage pregnancies, black-on-black crime, and the spread of AIDS from drug abuse and unprotected sexual relations, and help counter the despair, nihilism, and hopelessness that so starkly afflict our communities. Working together with other scholars, politicians, and activists who have developed these programs, we can begin to close the economic gap that divides the black community in two.

Dr. King did not die so that *half* of us would "make it," and *half* of us perish, forever tarnishing two centuries of struggle and agitation for our equal rights. We, the members of Du Bois's Talented Tenth, must accept our historical responsibility and live King's credo that none of us is free until each of us is free. And that all of us are brothers and sisters, in spirit—white and black, brown, red, and yellow, rich and poor black, Protestant and Catholic, Gentile, Jew, and Muslim, gay and straight—even if—to paraphrase Du Bois—we are not brothers- or sisters-in-law.

Henry Louis Gates, Jr.
Cornel West
Thanksgiving 1995

THE FUTURE OF THE RACE

PARABLE OF THE TALENTS

HENRY LOUIS GATES, JR.

In memory of
Glen DeChabert (1949–1994)
and
Armstead Robinson (1947–1995)

There is an historical circumstance, known to few, that connects the children of the Puritans with these Africans of Virginia in a very singular way. They are our brethren, as being lineal descendants from the Mayflower, *the fated womb of which, in her first voyage, sent forth a brood of Pilgrims on Plymouth Rock, and, in a subsequent one, spawned slaves upon the Southern soil,—a monstrous birth, but with which we have an instinctive sense of kindred, and are so stirred by an irresistible impulse to attempt their rescue, even at the cost of blood and ruin. The character of our sacred ship, I fear, may suffer a little by this revelation; but we must let her white progeny offset her dark one,—and two such portents never sprang from an identical source before.*

—NATHANIEL HAWTHORNE

There are so many privileges and immunities denied us as citizens, which we are entitled to enjoy equally with others, that we would be discouraged at the prospect of the long fight we have before us to secure them, if we did not stop to reflect that, by our history as well as the history of others, they only succeed who refuse to fail and who fight all the time for theirs whatever the obstacles. I feel that way about it now at the age of seventy-five as I did at the age of twenty-one. I want all the young and the old people of the race to feel about it in the same way.

—T. Thomas Fortune

The temptation therefore, to read the Negro out of the human family is exceedingly strong, and may account somewhat for the repeated attempts on the part of Southern pretenders to science, to cast a doubt over the Scriptural account of the origin of mankind. If the origin and motives of most works, opposing the doctrine of the unity of the human race, could be ascertained, it may be doubted whether one such work could boast an honest parentage. Pride and selfishness, combined with mental power, never want for a theory to justify them—and when men oppress their fellow-men, the oppressor ever finds, in the character of the oppressed, a full justification for his oppression. Ignorance and depravity, and the inability to rise from degradation to civilization and respectability, are the most usual allegations against the oppressed. The evils most fostered by slavery and oppression, are precisely those which slaveholders and oppressors would transfer from their system to the inherent character of their victims. Thus the very crimes of slavery become slavery's best defence. By making the enslaved a character fit only for slavery, they excuse themselves for refusing to make the slave a freeman.

—Frederick Douglass

HOW TO JOIN THE BLACK OVERCLASS

TWENTY-FIVE years ago, I left West Virginia for Yale University, to join the blackest class in the history of that ivy-draped institution. I drove up on my own, without my parents. They were never comfortable in that island of leaded glass and Gothic spires, although you might say they spent much of their lives making sure I arrived there. My father worked two jobs—loading trucks at a paper mill, plus a night shift as a janitor for the phone company—to keep us well fed and well clothed, and to pay the premiums on "college insurance policies," a thousand dollars when we reached eighteen. It never occurred to me that we might be poor until much later a sociologist told me so, pinpointing "the Gateses" in a mass of metallic-tasting demographics that left me numb with the neatness of it all.

I suppose that Yale represented both a betrayal and a fulfillment of their dreams. Blacks are wedded to narratives of ascent, to borrow a phrase from literary critic Robert Stepto, and we have made the compounded preposition "up from" our own: up from slavery, up from Piedmont, up from the Bronx, always up. But narratives of ascent, whether or not we like to admit it, are also narratives of alienation, of loss. Usually the ascent is experienced not as a gradual progression but as a leap, and for so many of my generation that leap was the one that took us from our black homes and neighborhoods into the white universities that had adopted newly vigorous programs of minority recruitment. It should be said that the adjustment was a two-way street: we were as strange to the institutions in which we found ourselves as those institutions were to us. In short, we were part of a grand social experiment—a blind date, of sorts. We weren't a tenth, of course; and whatever talent we had wasn't necessarily greater than our compeers who were passed over, or who opted out; but we were here. You might call us the crossover generation.

To speak in strictly chronological terms, we are among the late-boomers who now occupy the White House and the Congress—an age grade that includes Bill Clinton and Robert Reich and William Kristol. But the sense of generational affinity is intensified within the race: ours was the first generation to attend integrated schools in the wake of *Brown v. Board;* to have watched, as children, the dismantling of Jim Crow and to wonder where the process might end; to be given the chance, through affirmative action, to compete against white boys and girls; to enter and integrate the elite institutions just as the most expansive notions of radical democracy made an entrance.

I picked Yale almost out of a hat. After a year at a junior college near my home, a place where "nigger" was hung on me so many times that I thought it was my name, I decided to head north, armed with a scholarship and a first edition of Strunk and White's *The Elements of Style.*

By day—and it was still light when I first arrived in New Haven—the university is a tangible, mortar-and-stone manifestation of an Oxonian ideal of Gothic perfection. By night, the sense of enchantment increased:

the mammoth structures, strangely out of keeping with the surrounding town, guarded their streets with bearded shadows made by the half-light of the lamp-posts. At Yale, battle hymns were Congregational, with delicate changes of key. The building that just *had* to be the college cathedral turned out to be Sterling Library. Every feature of the place was alarming and exhilarating. Welcome to Never-Never Land, I told myself. This is your world, the world you've longed for and dreamed of. This was where the goods and entitlements of the American century were stored and distributed. It was the grown-up version of the world of Captain Midnight Decoders; the repository of all those box tops I used to ship off to Kellogg's in fair exchange for laser guns. If college was a warehouse for what we've modishly learned to call "cultural capital," the question wasn't how to get it but what to do with it.

Many of the black kids at Yale were the first in their families to attend college, and they congregated in the pre-med and pre-law tracks, searching for a secure place in the newly integrated arenas of the nation's elite. Others were scions of old "colored money." Most of us took at least one course in the new program in Afro-American Studies, probably in part out of a sense of team spirit, partly out of a yearning to tap our cultural unconscious. I took several such courses, and at least three times found myself assigned to read Du Bois's essay "The Talented Tenth." (Only Harold Cruse's *The Crisis of the Negro Intellectual* was assigned more often.) Du Bois's essay was read and critiqued, almost defensively, for its vanguardism; but its vision of the educated bourgeoisie as the truly revolutionary class—Marx stood on its head, you might say—exerted an unmistakable sway on us.

A PAIR OF ACES

AND THEN there was the talented tenth of the Talented Tenth: *la crème de la crème brûlée*. As far as I was concerned, they numbered exactly two: Glen DeChabert and Armstead Robinson. I first met them in the pages of the *Yale Alumni Magazine* the summer before I set foot on campus. In it was an article about a conference held at Yale on the prospective shape of Afro-American Studies in the academy—a conference, bringing together illustrious scholars and prominent activists, that had been orchestrated by these two Yale sophomores. (That conference, and the book that came out of it, would profoundly influence the institutionalization of the field; and indeed, the program in Afro-American Studies came to Yale the same year I did.) I studied their photographs. DeChabert seemed to have a cappuccino complexion, an aquiline nose, an impressive crown of hair, and a compellingly regal bearing: I was half convinced he was descended from African royalty. Robinson's customary attire was more in keeping with countercultural dishabille; he had wavy, unkempt hair in quantity and wore the black rectangular glasses that were then standard issue for young black activist-intellectuals.

Soon after my arrival, I attended my first meeting of the Black Student Alliance at Yale, at which Glen DeChabert—or DeCh, as he was called—presided in his capacity as "moderator." He was every bit as charismatic as I'd imagined, and I hung back like a supplicant. Besides, there was a lot to take in. I could only marvel when students complained that there weren't enough "brothers" on campus; looking around at the two hundred or so students in attendance, I felt as if I were in Africa, or Harlem, anyway. Outside of a few camp revival meetings in Moorefield, I'd never seen so many black people my age. I'd grown up in colored Piedmont; here I would truly learn how to be Black. If my arrival was a narrative of ascent, it was at the time one of immersion. Then it came up that they needed a new secretary. This was my cue. After the meeting, summoning my nerve, I pushed through a crowd of DeCh's admirers and volunteered my services. I felt anointed when he accepted. From then on, I took notes during meeting after meeting, participating through the sedulous act of recording. It's a role that I return to now with some trepidation, but I have no other way of explaining what is, in part, the story of my generation.

If DeChabert—with his impeccable attire and his lordly way with a cigarette—struck me as the perfect embodiment of black leadership, Armstead Robinson was an equally commanding picture of black intellection. Thin and ascetic in his unpressed dashiki and uncombed Afro, Robinson—Robby—was the first black "Scholar of the House," part of a competitive senior-year program in which a major scholarly project was pursued instead of regular course work. Robby, we knew, would change the way we understood our past and our present, by dint of his extraordinary and well-

7

stocked mind. He was the son of a Memphis minister, and his verbal facility was displayed to equal advantage in the high-flown language of the humanities and in the revolutionary lingo of the streets. Once I gained his friendship, I'd go over to his room at Morse College and sit on the floor cross-legged as he typed away. "I won't bother you," I'd tell him. "I just want to watch you work." The truth is that I was starstruck: I'd never met a black scholar before, and in some almost mystical way I wanted to witness the act of creation, hoping that the magic would rub off.

They respected each other, Robby and DeCh did, each ceding the other his turf. I remember when a number of representatives of the SDS came to campus and we were supposed to hold a "meeting with the white boys." DeCh couldn't go, and asked me to attend in his place, to report back. "I just want to know one thing," he'd said when I caught up with him afterward, lighting up a cigarette impatiently. "Was Robby there?"

Best of all, DeChabert was a man with a plan. A very practical-sounding plan. What black America needed, he often said, was economic development, and the only way that was going to happen was if we did it ourselves. Economies grew: that was what they did. And we were a nation of millions, more populous than Canada. Black capitalism was the answer, and he was going to be its Johnny Appleseed, lending out start-up capital for black entrepreneurship and reinvesting the proceeds until the relative deprivation of black America was a distant memory—and until it truly was a force to be reckoned with. Of course, he did recognize there was a long way to go.

LIFTED AS WE CLIMBED

IN THE YEAR I was born, 1950, 5 percent of employed blacks held professional or managerial jobs; another 5 percent held clerical or sales jobs. So, depending on the elasticity of your definition, maybe a tenth would have qualified as "middle-class." To spell out the obverse: Among even those blacks who held jobs, 90 percent failed, by conventional standards, to qualify as middle-class. If educational attainment was your measure, the situation looked bleaker; even ten years later, only 3 percent of blacks had a college degree. And more than half of blacks fell below the poverty line. In the year I graduated from high school, almost half of black households took in less than fifteen thousand dollars a year, in today's dollars; less than 6 percent took in more than fifty thousand.

Given such figures, the persistent strain of antipathy toward the black middle class might seem a phenomenon analogous to the curious strain of anti-Semitism in present-day Japan: a prejudice undeterred by the fact that, empirically speaking, its target is scarcely to be seen. "Aunt Jemima and Uncle Tom are dead," James Baldwin wrote, slyly, in 1955, "their places taken by a group of amazingly well-adjusted young men and women, almost as dark, but ferociously literate, well-dressed and scrubbed, who are never laughed at, who are not likely ever to set foot in a cotton or tobacco field or in any but the most modern of kitchens." Three years after *Brown,* in his classic 1957 study, *Black Bourgeoisie,* E. Franklin Frazier described his subject in the most withering terms, depicting them as deluded turncoats. With even more polemical zeal if less analytic precision, Nathan Hare's popular book *The Black Anglo-Saxons* (1965) presented the black bourgeoisie as servile, inauthentic, self-loathing, and generally contemptible. Where Du Bois saw saviors, a new generation saw only sellouts. Thus was the rhetorical template established, and you could feel its impress for years to come. Martin Luther King, Jr., charged that "many middle-class Negroes have forgotten their roots," and are "untouched by the agonies and struggles of their underprivileged brothers." Harold Cruse would later denounce "an empty class that has flowered into social prominence without a clearly defined social mission."[1] And of course the Black Arts generation, those merry pranksters, added their own flourishes. The folkloric figure Junebug Jabbo Jones was often quoted saying, "Yale done spoilt more good Negroes than whiskey." Self-loathing was held to be a trait of the black bourgeoisie; it did not occur to these authors that their own work might itself be evidence of it.

But if the full-fledged rise of black-bourgeois-bashing preceded the full-fledged rise of the black bourgeoisie, time soon rectified the imbalance. For however paltry the middle class was in absolute terms, these critics wrote in a period when the socioeconomic structure of black America was undergoing a dramatic transformation: during the forties, fifties, and sixties, the black middle class experienced what was then the most rapid growth in its history. Postwar prosperity was the wind at our back. Between 1940 and 1970, for example, the annual earnings of white men doubled; but those of black men actually tripled.

So it was a period when the belief in progress seemed more than wishful thinking. Certainly my parents never allowed my brother or me to doubt that we could become whatever we chose. Nor did they let us doubt that the world would yield its secrets if only we turned our attention to it. They were not surprised by their children's attainments. I do not know if they loved America, but they shared the hopeful vision of America that the Princeton political scientist Jennifer Hochschild has analyzed in an invaluable 1995 study as the ideology of the "American dream."[2] That is, they believed in the possibility of upward mobility, of racial betterment, of collective progress. They believed that America was in part malign, but that it was not entirely malign. They believed that the agency of black folk was circumscribed by circumstance, but that black folk had agency all the same. They knew that white folk had the power; but they believed that power was a shifting, fluid thing, like mercury, and that some of it was always seeping away, puddling up before somebody else. They knew that black folk had gone through bad times, but they also let themselves believe, or at least half-believe, that times they were a-changin'.

The vision of the world they shared was one in which both our purpose and our enemies were clear. We were to get just as much education as we possibly could, to stay the enemies of racism, segregation, and discrimination. (If we heard it once, we heard it a thousand times: education is the one thing nobody can take away from you.) By my first year of school, at the Davis Free School in Piedmont, West Virginia—which had integrated just one year before I entered—I understood in some deep part of me that all that was being asked of me was to pay attention. We never once were allowed to doubt that we were special. And only sometimes did we allow ourselves to wonder why.

It was a world in which comporting ourselves with dignity and grace, striving to "know and test the cabalistic letters" (as Du Bois put it) of the white elite— but also acknowledging and honoring those of us who had achieved—was central to being a colored person in America: so we were given to understand. And indeed, back when Du Bois was the editor of *The Crisis* magazine, he published the portraits of black college graduates, lawyers and doctors, on its cover and in its pages. Law and medicine, education and scholarship— these were the pinnacles of achievement, these the province of the Talented Tenth. I don't claim that we ever lived up to this idealized image. But at least these were the images, the ideals, that were presented to us. Once upon a time, our communal values and aspirations were intact. Only racism and segregation stood between our people and the fullness of American citizenship. If only we could secure our legal rights, the argument went, if only we could use the courts to strike down segregation; if only *de jure* segregation could be banished from the land once and for all—then all else would follow, as day upon night. The world was simple then; our enemy an easy target.

And then the obvious obstacles tumbled and fell. *De jure* segregation was killed off in the American judicial system. *Brown v. Board* was a triumph of decades of legal scholarship, under the leadership of such accomplished jurists as Charles Hamilton Houston, Thurgood Marshall, Constance Baker Motley—the list is long and noble. (How much went into the preparation of that brief before the Court—a rare collaboration between our legal practitioners and our scholars, between politicians and political activists, between whites and blacks, Jews and Gentiles, working together in an interracial compact that few of us can even remember, let alone imagine happening again.) Certainly the decade between *Brown* and the passage of the Voting Rights Act in 1965 was a time when the Negro felt more optimism than would have been justified in any other single decade in our century.

To be sure, the three years that followed were bloody and turbulent ones (you could think of these years as framed by the assassinations of Malcolm X and Martin Luther King, or by the riots in Watts in 1965 and the riots just about everywhere else in 1968, especially those surrounding the Democratic Convention in Chicago). And yet despite all this, the grandchildren of the Talented Tenth—those who had been trained to succeed, geared to prosper, prepared by family and teachers to "cross over" into the white world once the walls of segregation came tumbling down—plunged headlong into the abyss of integration. In the years between my graduation from high school and my graduation from college, the poorest fifth percentile of blacks experienced a 13 percent gain in income, about the same as the top fifth percentile. Here, at last, was the proverbial "rising tide" that lifts all boats, one that buoyed a sense of possibility shared by militants and assimilationists alike. How could we have known that we were never to see its like again?

EVEN IN ARCADIA

THE SORT of institutions through which elites sustain themselves always seemed to inhabit an arcadia of their own, and yet somehow, in my mind, they always loomed like the clanking, infernal machinery of Fritz Lang's *Metropolis*. I should say that Yale wasn't my first encounter with one. I was in tenth grade when Exeter came about; a friend at a church summer camp told me about the place. Going to Exeter, you understand, was not something people in Piedmont knew about, not the way people at Yale "know" about Exeter. What *I* knew was that it was a place with a big library which offered a lot of courses. And in the main, that's what it was for me. An interview with the young Jay Rockefeller, an easy entrance exam, and a full scholarship later, I said bye-bye to Piedmont and drove with my uncle to the New Hampshire woods. My parents said their good-byes in Piedmont, as if there were a boundary they preferred not to trespass.

As quickly as Exeter came into my life, however, Exeter left; or rather, I left Exeter. Sometime in my first semester, I "up and decided" that it was past time for me to go back home. Dean Kessler checked my records what seemed to be a hundred times—my test scores were perfect, I had straight A's. There was no reason, he said. "Who gave you authority to leave?" he wanted to know. That's what settled it for me. I thought the knock on the door was just my classmate Joel Motley, whose room was next to mine. It was the dean, red-faced, angry, and a bit disappointed. I think he thought if he yelled at me, somehow I would cower my way back to French 1-A. I gave up Exeter at that moment, staring blankly into his crimson, pockmarked face. "Think of our people," Joel, the soul of black insouciance, said that night. "Think of yourself. Where is Piedmont, anyway?" "I'll be back," I told him, and somehow knew I would, though I didn't mean Exeter, exactly. That was the first airplane trip I ever took. I still don't know for sure why I felt I had to leave; I think that Piedmont was just too far to fall back into, so I decided not to have to fall at all. Homesick for Piedmont, I went back, and soon became homesick for Exeter.

But I stayed at Yale; DeChabert and Robinson were my polestars, and would keep me from ever getting lost. I stayed and I graduated, as a number of my friends did not, and I did so not as a matter of course but as a matter of will. I still remember that crucial first month, with daily sessions in the Linnonia and Brothers reading room, working out inorganic chemistry problems by the light of the low-wattage table lamps. I had convinced myself that at Yale I would be average; a C+ was what I was aiming for. Learning to speak out in class, always my forte before, now came slowly and painfully. But it was History 31 that made the difference, in Burrell Billingslea's discussion group. Never have I put so much work and expectation, fear and care, into the preparation of a five-page paper. Had the returned grade been a Pass, or just a High Pass, the tenor of my years at Yale would probably have been as gray as a New Haven winter. But there it was, in unforgettable bright red letters: "Honors. Nice Paper." Fifteen students—eight seniors, four juniors, and a handful of others—and one Honors. I remember deciding that very night to go tó Africa the next year as a "Five-Year B.A.," and one day to be a Scholar of the House, just like Robby.

It soon became apparent, once the anxiety of "making it" was allayed, and once the sheer joy at being black (with about two hundred other black folks!) was tempered, that the fundamental challenge of my years at Yale would be whether or not to allow blackness to rob me of what I wistfully and portentously called "my humanity." This problem went beyond, I think, that peculiar brand of "Mau-Mauing" we so avidly practiced during the late 1960s. You see, as long as I identified the angst of youth with discovering and then shouting for all to hear just how the white man had subjugated the black man, then the matter of being a human being was not a problem at all. (Try it sometime.)

But it was only when you put aside the hulking specter of Bull Connors, arms folded before the passageway, that you would be *made* to confront all those inconvenient matters. So if you were no longer sure about who you were, it was awfully convenient to have a Bull Connors for distraction. Maybe that explained part of the strange spectacle we presented at Yale, preoccupying ourselves with the minute examination of the metaphysical nature of the "Pig." We wanted to dissect his brain, to explicate his soul, each of us determined at all costs to unlink the Great Chain of Being that had enslaved us since 1619. How better to serve our people, then, than as students at an elite institution? "Changing the system by knowing just what the system is"—that was our rationale, a rationale that was recited so rotely and smugly that the white kids stopped asking us the sort of questions that might prompt it—questions like whether we "felt guilty about just *being* here." That was the sort of question we would not even have answered in private, among ourselves behind closed doors or alone; we certainly would not have been frank with the white boys. So it was another device by which to mystify them, and mask our own fears.

Not everything was fantasy and posture; in 1970, certainly, the issues of the day were real enough. There was Bobby Seale in a New Haven prison, tried each day in a courthouse just a half-block from Calhoun College; there was Eldridge Cleaver, unjustly exiled in Algiers; there was John Huggins, whose mother would sometimes let our fines slide over at the Sterling Library, murdered by cultural nationalists out in L.A.; there were the atrocities of the Cambodian "sideshow." None of these issues was conjured up for the occasion; our growing conviction was that such were the evils against which only a moral elite of the young could prevail. Yet throughout all our strikes and protests and steering committees, I tried to shrug off a vague sense that had these things not been there, in the world, we would have invented them; or at least a sense that these things were doing double-duty for us.

My grandfather was colored, my father is Negro, and I am black—so I wrote in my college application essay. Those appellations, of course, did not contain who I was, or even serve to limit who I thought I could be. Yet each successive generation of black folks living in this country has shared certain peculiar psychic and social concerns that come as regularly as dusk in a society where being black was from the start a restrictive covenant that one could run from or live with, but that one could not escape. It was always a fact of Negro life that one's membership could be taken for granted, could be assumed in much the same way one could assume that back home those Saturday sessions at Combie's barbershop would be rife with Combie's "boo-shit" and with the good-hearted lies that provoked it. As my understanding grew of just what all the post-1966 Black Power rhetoric meant, of just how ideology could come to bear upon personal, everyday relationships, I came to the painful realization that what "da revolution" implied, what that elusive vanguard was based on, was membership in a club so exclusive that, as one for whom the warmth of a village was sustenance, I couldn't begin to afford its ideological membership fee.

Not long after I arrived at Yale, some of the brothers who came from private schools in New Orleans held a "bag party." As a classmate explained it to me, a bag party was a New Orleans custom wherein a brown paper bag was stuck on the door and anyone darker than it was denied entrance. That was one cultural legacy that would be put to rest in a hurry—we all made sure of that. But in a manner of speaking, it was replaced by an opposite test whereby those who were deemed "not black enough," ideologically, were to be shunned. I was not so sure this was an improvement.

THE TIMOROUS TENTH

THE YEAR I graduated from college, 1973, marked the beginning of a growing divergence between poor blacks and prosperous ones, such that the well-off became better-off while the poor became poorer; and in the years since, poverty has, in lockstep, kept pace with privilege. First, though, the good news. Today, roughly a third of black families can be counted as middle-class. I've mentioned that in 1950, only 5 percent of black workers were professionals or managers; today, the figure is greater than 20 percent. The number of black families earning more than fifty thousand dollars a year has quadrupled since 1967, and doubled in the eighties alone. In 1973, the top one hundred black-owned businesses had sales of $473 million; today, the figure is $11.7 billion. In 1970, only one in ten blacks had attended college; today, one in three has.

The black middle class has never been in better shape—and it has never felt worse about things. Du Bois had conjured up a Talented Tenth that would be a beacon of hope; it is ninety years later, and they are, instead, a sump of gloom. Middle-class messianism has given way to middle-class malaise. Jennifer Hochschild, the political scientist, calls this paradox "succeeding more and enjoying it less."

Certainly the data she has assembled are striking. Over the past generation, poor and affluent black Americans have switched places with respect to their attitudes toward America and their expectations of economic progress and of the future of race relations; the result is a kind of ideological chiasmus. Professor Hochschild writes:

> When asked what is important for getting ahead in life, poor blacks are almost as likely to choose being of the right sex and more likely to choose religious conviction and political connections than to choose being of the right race. Well-off blacks, however, think race matters more than any of those characteristics. Affluent blacks are also more likely to see blacks are economically worse off than whites, and to see discrimination as blacks' most important problem. . . . As the African American middle class has become larger, more powerful, and more stable, its members have grown disillusioned with and even embittered about the American dream.[3]

This represents a dramatic reversal of the situation during the years of my childhood, in the fifties and sixties. In 1964, 70 percent of middle-class blacks surveyed said they thought most whites want to see blacks get a better break; by 1992, only 20 percent thought so. The Talented Tenth has a surprising susceptibility to racial paranoia, too: blacks with a college education are especially likely to seriously entertain claims that AIDS was concocted to infect blacks, or that the government conspired to make drugs available in poor neighborhoods in an effort to harm blacks. Material success has led to the death of trust. In short, even as the numbers of the affluent have swollen, the hopefulness of the affluent has plunged. Antonio Gramsci, famously, recommended pessimism of the intellect and optimism of the will; for much of the black elite, pessimism has prevailed on both fronts.

Why should this be? We're certainly free to speculate. Some critics would probably implicate the oppositional culture of the sixties, as incubated in the very elite institutions that secured us a place among the educated bourgeoisie. It isn't unknown for an oppositional creed to decay into a kind of routinized cynicism. Then there's the fact that economic advancement entails greater intimacy with whites, and so greater opportunities for friction. You might even wonder about the effects of stigmatizing black upward mobility; certainly the figure of the inauthentic buppy has passed from the sociological study into popular black films and novels. Culturally speaking, the "street" has been deemed the repository of all that is real, that is "black," and alternative models of ethnic solidarity have been late in coming. But probably more significant is the matter of dashed hopes: of great expectations, and the mourning after.

THINGS FALL APART

HERE, YOU have to contend both with a story of political retrenchment and the very real phenomenon of survivor's guilt. The story of retrenchment has been told many times, but these are its lineaments. The New Deal cemented a popular coalition that was supportive of the newly institutionalized welfare state: it spoke a universalist language of equal opportunity, fairness, and civic-minded virtue. But, we have been told, the ultimate ascension of that vision contained the seeds of its demise. Return, then, to the sixties. In what would become known as the "Great Society speech," delivered on May 22, 1964, President Lyndon B. Johnson spoke of a civilization where "the city of man serves not only the needs of the body and the demands of commerce but the desire for beauty and the hunger for community . . . where the demands of morality, and the needs of the spirit, can be realized in the life of the nation." And with these lofty words, he launched the most ambitious agenda of social and economic reform since the New Deal.

Of course, the New Deal, which bequeathed us what we know as modern liberalism, was patched together in a time of economic crisis, impelled by desperation. By contrast, Johnson's vision was buoyed by the prosperity of the time, fueled by a national mood of expansiveness. If America's capacity for self-improvement was not inexhaustible, our faith in that capacity surely was. That November, Johnson was returned to office by what was the largest popular margin in history. But it is the long shadow and the troubled legacy of the Great Society—not its policy failures so much as its *political* failure—with which his successors have had to grapple. (Many saw Clinton's election as signaling a renewal of the old Democratic alliance, the one that the Great Depression put together and the sixties put asunder. The years that followed have not been kind to that hopeful belief.)

The early days of the Great Society witnessed a host of legislative initiatives. There was Medicare for the elderly, Medicaid for the indigent, Head Start for preschoolers. There was the Elementary and Secondary Education Act, the Job Corps, the Model Cities program. Of greater political significance was the promulgation and enforcement of sweeping civil rights measures, such as the Civil Rights Act of 1964 and the Voting Rights Act of 1965. Through five heady years, the Great Society seemed to embody the full and resplendent maturity of liberalism, fending off the forces of reaction and ushering in a bright new day.

In the ensuing decades, it came to look a lot more like liberalism's supernova: a final, white-hot burst before its dark collapse.

As with the New Deal, some of the programs were poorly conceived and ineffectual. Others are now taken for granted as a part of the political biosphere, programs whose worth neither party would dare contest. But it was the overarching scheme, and dream, that fell into disfavor. Reform was no longer experienced as something performed for the people, but as something performed *on* the people. In an age of belated racial redress, white America—the rank and file, the lower middle class—felt itself to be under siege. With jolting suddenness, the old alliance fell apart. Liberalism was coded as a philosophy elevating black grievances over white ones, concerned with the welfare of layabouts over that of workers.

The irony was that liberalism, which sought to heal the injuries of class, should itself fall victim to class warfare—to the resentment of the blue-collar and lower-middle classes against those they saw as the professional-class purveyors of paternalism. White Southerners and Northern ethnics, once Democratic stalwarts, increasingly felt like outsiders at the gate. A Great Society? Not if you'd been left off the invitation list. Liberalism lost its political capital when it became perceived as something that taxed the majority to advance "special"—which is to say "minority"—interests. Through an excess of gallantry and zeal, liberalism itself created the alienated "them" that deeded the Republicans the White House.[4]

The upshot is that the members of the crossover generation—the black boomers—have kept vigil over the increasing marginalization of black America in the political arena. Now Democrats win national office by demonstrating that they are not beholden to black "special interests," while Republicans have mastered a nimble vocabulary for reassuring white voters that they're on their side.

THE POVERTY PERPLEX

WHAT MAKES all this of particular concern is the swelling ranks of the black poor, a category that (like the black middle class) now encompasses about a third of black families. More than half of all black males between twenty-five and thirty-four are jobless or "underemployed." Other social indices are equally discouraging: In 1993, 2.3 million black men were sent to jail or prison while 23,000 received a college diploma—a ratio of a hundred to one. (The ratio for whites was six to one.) And the plight of the black poor is even more alarming if you look not just at household earnings but at assets. The poorest fifth of whites have a median net worth of ten thousand dollars; the median net worth of their black counterparts is . . . zero.

On a rational level, of course, we know that black prosperity doesn't derive from black poverty; on a symbolic level, however, the chronic hardship of a third of black America is a standing reproach to those of us who once dreamed of collective uplift. It makes it hard to invoke the salvific conception of the "Talented Tenth" without bitterness. If your name is Auchincloss, say, you do not worry overmuch about those impoverished Appalachians who share your Scottish descent; few blacks have the luxury of such detachment.

Du Bois once believed that educated Negroes would uplift the race; give or take a few revolutionary flourishes, most of my black classmates at college would have concurred. It *sounded* different, our creed, but it came to the same thing. So it's easy to take our collective misfortunes personally. Forty years after *Brown v. Board,* most black students attend majority black schools; a third attend schools that are 90 to 100 percent black. Everything was supposed to have been different from the way it turned out.

The sixties bequeathed us new and inventive ways of talking about race, thus presenting us with a

chimera called the "black community." And sometimes, to be sure, solidarity was conjured into existence—at least a provisional existence. In 1970, a day
before the legendary May Day rally in New Haven, I
noticed two Black Panthers leaving my entryway at
Calhoun "College," as the undergraduate dorms are
known. Brimming with the spirit of brotherly bonding,
I introduced myself to them. Panthers *were* glamorous
creatures, after all—the shock troops of our belea-
guered nation. I told them my name and, for their future reference, my room number. They looked at each
other uneasily. I understood why a little later that
evening, when they knocked on the door, bearing my
yellow windbreaker, my copy of Bobby Seale's *Seize
the Time,* and *Karma,* the Pharoah Sanders album—
all items they had stolen from my room earlier. I hadn't
noticed their absence, and I felt oddly touched by their
return. I suppose I didn't know whether this was a
parable of brotherhood or of the limits of brotherhood. It was not an uncommon quandary.

In the event, we lost our grip on things like class,
and felt ill equipped to deal with the dilemma of *in-
tra*racial disparities. Twenty-five years later, we can't
even agree on the causes of black poverty, let alone
how best to remedy it. Of course, we do have theories—so many that, as Mr. Dooley says, "you pays
your money and you takes your choice." There is, for
example, the "spatial-mismatch hypothesis," which
holds that while manufacturing jobs moved to the suburbs, blacks (in part deterred by residential discrimination and the inadequacies of mass transit) have stayed
behind in the central cities.[5] (This explanation can be

summed up in the expression: the wrong place at the wrong time.) There's a school of opinion that emphasizes the malign effects of the concentration of poverty that arises from residential segregation. It turns out that, much more than the poor of other backgrounds, the black poor are concentrated in uniformly disadvantaged neighborhoods, and, it's proposed, such concentration itself has a pernicious impact on life opportunities.[6] There are those who stress the deindustrialization of the American economy over the past several decades, and the resultant loss of entry-level blue-collar jobs—the sort of jobs that had provided other groups with an economic stepping-stone.[7] Still others dwell on the disintegration of the traditional family structure and the rise of female-headed households (sometimes naming AFDC as an aggravating factor). You can, of course, mix and match these theories, and to varying degrees, most researchers do.

No doubt all these trends have played a role—but how significant a role? With respect to "spatial mismatch," you might think that if blacks were able to secure good-paying jobs at suburban businesses, they would be able to afford the commute; after all, *most* blue-collar workers drive to work. As Christopher Jencks, a leading analyst of social policy, argues, "At least for mature men most metropolitan areas constitute a single labor market, not separate urban and suburban markets."[8] One problem with research on the concentration of poverty is how to factor in the presumably positive position enjoyed by those blacks whose departure from the central cities created those vexing concentrations. Skeptics armed with longitudinal studies note that the deindustrialization of American cities is a trend that began early in the century and its progress doesn't seem to mirror the fluctuating fortunes of the black working class. For that matter, the rate of single motherhood has proven insensitive to changes in welfare policy—that is, the rate has risen when welfare benefits rose; and also risen when benefits were cut back or qualification requirements made more stringent. In any event, there is a chicken-and-egg problem here: the increase in female-headed households may be a consequence of the problems—such as black joblessness—it is supposed to explain. (One factor I haven't mentioned is the most obvious: contemporary race discrimination per se. Such discrimination persists, needless to say; but there's little agreement about how large a role it plays. That black women now earn about the same as white women of comparable education, many believe, indicates that skin color alone is not determinative. Plainly the political economy of race and poverty has to be responsive to the lingering effects of historical inequity—which argues for a concept of "racism without racists.")

In the bluffly empirical sense that the root cause of poverty is a lack of money, however, what ails us isn't a failure of analysis but a failure of national will. The politics of poverty is more vexed than the economics of it. The sociologist Herbert J. Gans, a veteran of the welfare wars, maintains:

Antipoverty programs have rarely been costed out to determine their benefits, such as what people employed in newly created jobs return to the tax rolls, what job and income grant programs save in spending for controlling and reducing crime and the physical and mental illnesses associated with poverty. If all the externalities, good and bad, associated with spending by and for (or against) the poor were added together, they would show that the country can afford far better antipoverty programs than it now provides.

And the fact that federal welfare expenditures have never amounted to more than a percentage or two of the federal budget lends credibility to his view. Gans notes that the total cost of welfare and food stamps in 1992 was $47 billion, and he cites a Census Bureau finding that with another $37 billion, the incomes of all poor families with children could be raised to the poverty line.[9] One reason for the electoral reluctance to pony up is the enduring ideology of the "undeserving poor." Another is that poverty in this country wears a black face; it is true that most welfare recipients are white, but the disproportionate number of blacks below the poverty line creates the perception. All of which returns us to the story of the decline and fall of the New Deal coalition, and the continuing electoral allergy to race-specific programs.

Faced with these realities, many liberal social scientists have responded by advocating programs that unite black and white in a common purpose, steering clear of race-specific, even need-specific remedies, in favor of universal social policies. Take, for example, provisions for job training, universal health care coverage, access to college loans, apprenticeships for those who aren't college-bound. These are proposals whose potential beneficiaries, and therefore supporters, aren't restricted to the poor. Not incidentally, however, they are of particular value to the poor. None of these things looks like a "poverty program." All would help combat poverty. (It was conservative Chicago School economists like Gary Becker who first hit upon the notion of "human capital," the notion that education was an investment, like any other capital investment, only more profitable. A recent survey by two Princeton econometricians found that every additional year of education increased income by an average of 16 percent. If so, expanding the availability of education is just a smart investment, and should be promoted as one.) You may have noticed, however, that even proposals designed to have transracial appeal are regularly foiled by partisanship. The Clinton administration's attempts to implement such programs have met little success; and the Republican majority in Congress has guaranteed that the impasse will continue. Reform designed to promote work, not dependence—involving measures to promote, or at least not to penalize, savings—would cost more than conventional transfer payments, no question. Yet at least in the long run, there's reason to think that Americans, who are skeptical of handouts, could be persuaded to shell out more if it were spent in ways they approve of.

The Earned Income Tax Credit (EITC) is an example of a redistributive mechanism that, in the normal course of things, flies beneath the ideological radar. It is designed to be immune to the usual conservative worries about wrong-way incentives (the inevitable phaseout dilemmas aside) and about coddling the "undeserving poor": it rewards the poor for working by "making work pay," as the shibboleth has it. (The rub, of course, is that you need to find work first.) At the very least, you cannot claim that EITC perpetuates a "cycle of dependency." As Joel Handler, a law professor at UCLA, notes, the version that was enacted in 1992 would, when fully funded, redirect $7 billion a year, and save about fourteen million working poor families from poverty.[10] (Naturally, the program has been targeted for rescission by the Republican Congress.) Meantime, the entitlement spending currently represented by Social Security amounts to $333 billion each year; its beneficiaries include such people as Warren Buffett and David Rockefeller. With the money saved by implementing even an extremely conservative level of means-testing of Social Security recipients, the number of EITC beneficiaries could easily be doubled. In the absence of a political consensus, however, there is little point to playing the "if only" game of distributive justice. As the borscht-belt line has it: if we had bacon, we could have bacon and eggs—if we had eggs.

LEAD US NOT INTO TEMPTATION

BUT IN THE absence of a political establishment willing or able to address the crisis facing black America—in the absence, politically speaking, of both bacon and eggs—Du Boisian vanguardism proposes that we turn to our own black leadership to point the way. A recent article in *Black Enterprise,* for example, extolled the advantages of increased political representation at the municipal level, citing Atlanta, which has widely been viewed as a model of black empowerment. In Atlanta, we're told, "Mayor Jackson, and later Mayor Andrew Young, made sure African Americans got a fair share of city business. This helped black businesses grow. It also helped African Americans get jobs in law firms and led to the establishment of several black investment firms."[11] In short, a rising tide; lifted boats. But as Gary Orfield and Carole Ashkinaze have shown in a book-length case study of the city, working-class blacks did not share in its economic growth. "If economic expansion and a tight labor market could create equal opportunity without targeted government action, it should have happened in the Atlanta area," they write.[12] In fact, inner-city blacks were shut out of the emerging job market, which was largely to be found in outlying areas, and which drew upon workers from outside their neighborhoods.

But I should be fair. For every fatuous booster, there's a band of sad-eyed prophets bewailing the so-called leadership crisis in black America. And to judge by recent headlines, their lament has a certain plausibility. The NAACP finds an energetic new director—who soon resigns under a cloud. The freshman congressman Mel Reynolds, a onetime Rhodes scholar who won his Chicago seat in 1992 by defeating the odious incumbent, Gus Savage, is convicted of sexual misconduct. Mike Espy, Clinton's secretary of agriculture, announces, under pressure, that he will resign. Just as telling as the names of the preterites are those in the ascent. Marion Barry, having been convicted on drug charges, is returned to office as the mayor of Washington. And in Washington, Minister Louis Farrakhan takes center stage, having convened the best-attended black gathering in the nation's history. The mighty have fallen; the fallen have become mighty.

And so the hand-wringing and the talk about the crisis of leadership. If only we could get *that* part right—some blacks have started to think—we could start to get a handle on the grassroots problems. The trouble is, no one can agree on what that leadership should look like; no one ever could.

Pollsters have long known of the remarkable gap between the leaders and the led in black America. A 1985 survey found that most blacks favored the death penalty and prayer in public schools while most black leaders opposed these things. Most blacks opposed school busing, while most black leaders favored it. Three times as many blacks opposed abortion rights as their leaders did. Indeed, on many key social issues, blacks are more conservative than whites. If the numbers of black Republicans are on the rise, as these opinion surveys suggest, it would be unwise to dismiss the phenomenon. Given the breach between the black leadership and its putative constituency, we shouldn't be surprised at the motley company who seek to fill it.

In the early years of this century, black leadership was divided into two supposedly irreconcilable camps, the "integrationists" and the "accommodationists," with Du Bois and Booker T. Washington serving as exemplars and chief spokesmen for these two schools of thought. Where Du Bois called for an agenda of civil rights to be secured by the political and legal transformation of American society, Washington championed a form of group uplift to be secured by vocational education, with civil rights something to be dealt with down the road. With the coming of the civil rights era, and the partial fulfillment of Du Bois's agenda, the contending school of accommodationism was replaced by that of black separatism; Marcus Garvey, of the Back-to-Africa movement, and, later, Elijah Muhammad, of the Nation of Islam, squared off against civil rights organizations like the NAACP, CORE, the SCLC, and the National Urban League. Farrakhan's rhetoric sounds remote enough from Booker T. Washington's in tone, but they're cousins with respect to content.

The thornier issue, no doubt, is the matter of who counts as a black leader—and this, of course, depends on who's doing the counting. For decades now, *Ebony* magazine—still the only magazine to which many black families subscribe—has presented a list of "The 100 Most Influential Black Americans." As recently as 1970, *Ebony*'s list was a remarkably inclusive one. Just as you'd expect, the list that year included elected politicians, such as Senator Edward Brooke, Congresswoman Shirley Chisholm, and Newark mayor Ken Gibson, as well as various presidential appointees and judges. But the list also included radical luminaries, such as Huey P. Newton, Bobby Seale, Angela Davis, and Elijah Muhammad. It included poets, such as Imamu Amiri Baraka and Gwendolyn Brooks; athletes, such as John Mackey and Muhammad Ali; entertainers, such as James Brown, Bill Cosby, Duke Ellington, and Dick Gregory; scholars and writers, such as John Hope Franklin and Lerone Bennett; and businessmen, such as Berry Gordy and John Johnson, the publisher of *Ebony* himself. Then there were the leaders of black fraternal and sorority groups, with the colorful titles typical of such organizations—the Grand Exalted Ruler of the Elks, the Sovereign Grand Commander (South and North) of the Prince Hall Masons, the Grand Polemarch of Kappa Alpha Psi, and the Supreme Basileus of Alpha Kappa Alpha.

But as the Voting Rights Act gradually ushered in an unprecedented number of elected officials, the competition for spaces on the *Ebony* 100 grew keener, so that in recent years the list has been overrun by elected officials: typically around 40 percent of it is taken up with the names of U.S. representatives. Which is to say that the list has become more like a black version of Washington's "Blue Book" than the multifarious sampling of black opinion leaders it had once been. To make room for all those beltway types, in 1995 *Ebony* added a list of thirty-four "Organization Leaders" in which the Grand Basileus and the Grand Polemarch can now easily be found.

It isn't just in the pages of *Ebony* that the definition of black leadership has been mired in confusion. In 1994, Ben Chavis organized a controversial series of "leadership conferences," and it was interesting to note how few of the current *Ebony* 100 appeared on Chavis's list of leaders—and how fewer still attended his "leadership summit." Chavis's idea of leadership was clearly informed by a certain nostalgia for the sixties and for the intoxicating rhetoric of black nationalism. Hence he eagerly gathered together the aging remnants of a bygone era's nationalist vanguard, the sort of people the Black Student Alliance at Yale used to invite to campus in my day. He had the poets and activists Haki Madhubuti and Sonia Sanchez, the Black Power theorist and former leader of United Slaves Maulana Karenga, and, representing a somewhat younger generation, CCNY's professor Leonard Jeffries. Chavis, whose historical point of reference remains the Black Power era, attempted to define the current crisis of the black community along the hoary old assimilationist/separatist divide.

Certainly the rhetoric of defiance, such as Chavis favored, has been shown to conceal a multitude of sins. A several-term black representative told the political scientist Carol Swain: "One of the advantages, and disadvantages, of representing blacks is their shameless loyalty. You can almost get away with raping babies and be forgiven. You don't have *any* vigilance about your performance." No doubt this overstates the case, but it is a lesson that the likes of Adam Clayton Powell knew as well as Al Sharpton or Marion Barry. Such rhetoric is fueled by disenchantment; its only limitation is that it does nothing to remedy the disenchantment.

And yet a politics of solidarity—of unity, of "sacred covenants"—of the sort that both Representative Kweisi Mfume and Ben Chavis conjure in their speeches must inevitably run up against the hard facts of political economy. Hovering over the national conversation on the subject of black leadership is an implicit vision of thirty-five million black Americans as constituting a community of interests. But as we've seen, black America isn't just as fissured as white America; it is more so. And the mounting intraracial disparities mean that the realities of race no longer affect all blacks in the same way. There have been perverse consequences: in part to assuage our sense of survivor's guilt, we often cloak these differences in a romantic black nationalism—something that has become the veritable socialism of the black bourgeoisie.

But the easy Manichaeanism of the 1960s serves us poorly in the 1990s. In college, we believed that a politics could be buttressed by the idea of "blackness," an idea that was itself buttressed by an overarching system of social and legal racism; and in those days, that politics could efface a multitude of human differences. But this rhetoric has not kept pace with a changing reality. Although the Voting Rights Act served, in some measure, to ethnicize the notion of black electoral representation, its consequences would undermine the very premises of racial representation: the notion of a transparency of interests between the representative and the represented. Even today, however, the enormous class disparities within the "black community" are discussed only gingerly and awkwardly, and that's because they undermine the very concept of such a "community" in the first place.

Black cultural nationalism—make no mistake about it—is the figure in the carpet within African-American society. Appeals to nationalism—and, at the extreme fringes, to anti-Semitism, homophobia, and sexism—are drawn upon to mask class differences within the black community. As economic differences increase, the need to maintain the appearance of cultural and ideological conformity also increases. But it is these fake masks of conformity that disguise how very vast black class differentials really are. And no amount of kinte cloth or Kwanzaa celebrations will change this.

The real crisis in black leadership, then, is that the very idea of black leadership is in crisis. On this score, we can't turn for help to our vested elites—not even to our Grand Polemarches and Supreme Basileuses. For black America needs a politics whose first mission isn't the reinforcement of the idea of black America; and a discourse of race that isn't centrally concerned with preserving the idea of race and racial unanimity. We need something we don't yet have: a way of speaking about black poverty that doesn't falsify the reality of black advancement; a way of speaking about black advancement that doesn't distort the enduring realities of black poverty. I'd venture that a lot depends on whether we get it.

THE BLACK ARTS

WHICH IS not to say you should hold your breath. Literary neo-Marxists like to talk about the way that contradictions within the "social real" are apt to be resolved in the "realm of the aesthetic." It's a flossier version of the bad times/good art dialectic: the consolation-prize theory of artistic production. What's clear is that the influence of black America is less to be found in the electoral arena than in the cultural one. For all that African Americans have been shunted to the margins of national politics, they've resurfaced in the cultural mainstream.

There is a sort of logic to this. Disaffection, alienation, opposition: this is the very air that most artists and intellectuals breathe. Yet even to speak of the cultural mainstreaming of black America can be misleading. The point isn't that there are black artists and intellectuals who matter; it's that so many of the artists and intellectuals who matter are black. It's not that the cultural cutting edge has been influenced by black creativity; it's that black creativity, it so often seems today, *is* the cultural cutting edge. With choreographers such as Judith Jamison and Bill T. Jones, modern dance has pirouetted to new levels of expressivity. Musicians and composers such as Wynton Marsalis, Anthony Braxton, and Anthony Davis have recharged contemporary "concert" music with a fresh sense of mission—even as hip-hop has gone from being an underground sound to something like the American Bandstand of the 1990s. Novelists such as Nobel laureate Toni Morrison and John Edgar Wideman, and poets such as Rita Dove and Yusef Komunyakaa, both Pulitzer Prize winners, have explored the contours of literary language, while a whole new audience for black fiction has been galvanized by the more accessible company of Terry McMillan and Walter Mosley. Meanwhile, in the fine arts, figures like Martin Puryear, Lorna Simpson, and Carrie Mae Weems have produced an art that isn't simply "political," but that doesn't pretend to be innocent of politics, either. In a more populist vein, the bold vision of filmmakers like Spike Lee, Allen and Albert Hughes, Julie Dash, and John Singleton has arrested the attention of moviegoers—real ones, not just high-minded cineasts. George C. Wolfe's appointment as director of the New York Public Theater seems only to reinforce the impression that many of the most vibrant contributors to the American stage (among them August Wilson and Anna Deavere Smith) are black.

And the current flowering of black art and culture —with its inherent schisms and tensions—is unfolding against a conflicting socioeconomic backdrop. For despite remarkable gains, a sense of precariousness haunts this new black middle class, and the art that it creates and consumes. Its own economic advancement remains newfound and insecure.[13] Hence its peculiar love-hate attitude to the defiant cultural vistas of the inner city—an anxious amalgam of intimacy and enmity. Beneath it all is the black bourgeoisie's deep-seated fear that they're only a couple of paychecks away from the fate of the underclass. The nature and size of this new black middle class is significant here because of what it says about patronage and the economics of black art: whereas the Harlem Renaissance writers were almost totally dependent upon the whims of white patrons who marketed their works to a predominantly white readership, the sales of some of the most phenomenally successful black authors (such as Terry McMillan, Maya Angelou, Toni Morrison, and Alice Walker) are being sustained to an unprecedented degree by black readers. The rise of a black middle class, a black reading public, has fueled the new prominence of the black novel. And black novelists—especially the black women novelists—seem to owe a large part of their appeal to their capacity to express the desires and anxieties of this new middle class freely and from the inside. Then there are the institutional factors. For the first time, we have a significant presence of black agents, black editors, black reviewers. Blacks now run and own record labels. They produce films, back concerts. The old black talent/white management pattern has finally started to break down. With the active recruitment of minorities into the mainstream, blacks have an institutional authority without precedent in American cultural history.

Critics date the current efflorescence of black creativity variously, but many trace its genesis to the resurgence of black women's literature and criticism in the early eighties, especially the works of Ntozake Shange, Michele Wallace, Alice Walker, and Toni Morrison. These women, and their successors, were able both to reach the traditional large readership, which is by convention middle-class, white, and female, and a new black female audience that had been largely untapped, and unaddressed. The growth of this community of readers has resulted in an unprecedented number of black women's novels since 1980, as well as an unprecedentedly large black market for books about every aspect of the African-American experience.

Assigning a date to this upsurge in creativity is an exercise in arbitrariness, but the year 1987 will do as well as any. That was when August Wilson's *Fences* premiered on Broadway and Toni Morrison published *Beloved*. Both would receive Pulitzer Prizes. In that same year, PBS aired Henry Hampton's *Eyes on the Prize*, the six-part civil rights era documentary, Cornell scholar Martin Bernal published *Black Athena*, a controversial, revisionist history of the African origins of classical Greek civilization, and black pride slogans began to appear on T-shirts across the nation. The rap revolution, too, was reaching the heights of popularity it has since continued to enjoy.

Today's black arts scene is characterized by an awareness of previous black traditions, which these artists echo, imitate, parody, and revise, self-consciously, in acts of "riffing" or "signifying," or even "sampling." This concern with the black cultural past, and the self-conscious grounding of a black postmodernism in a black nationalist tradition, are accompanied by a certain nostalgia for the Black Power cultural politics of the sixties and the blaxploitation films of the early seventies. Unlike in that period, however, the current cultural movement has come to define itself by its openness—a cultural glasnost. Hence a zest for parodies and an impatience with sacred cows (as with George C. Wolfe's play *The Colored Museum,* or Rusty Cundieff's movie *Fear of a Black Hat,* a satire of hip-hop posturing). "What defines this renaissance, unlike the others," the novelist Jamaica Kincaid says, "is that people like us are just getting started. It is as if someone has removed the hands from over our mouths, and you hear this long, piercing scream." You hear a lot of other things, too—and some sound a lot like laughter. As the old Marxist saw has it, history repeats itself: the first time is tragedy, the second is farce.

This is an art that thrives on uncertainty, like much of the work of our postmodernist times, but it's also characterized by its confidence in the legitimacy of black experiences as artistic material. Forty-odd years ago, Richard Wright predicted that if "the Negro merges into the main stream of American life, there

might result actually a disappearance of Negro literature—as such." As a Negro, he continued, he was "a
rootless man." Few black writers today would agree
with Wright on either point. Today, black artists seem
to have become more conscious of the particularities of
their cultural traditions rather than less so. Discarding
the anxieties of a bygone era, these artists *presume* the
universality of the black experience.

They also know that the facts of race don't exhaust
anybody's human complexity. Indeed, much of the fiction being created by black women is coming-of-age
tales in which racial politics takes second place to the
unfolding of a sensitive, sexualized consciousness.
Today, a politicized naturalism is more likely to be
found in black film (such as John Singleton's *Boyz 'n
the Hood*) and, of course, in rap music like Public
Enemy's didactic "It Takes a Nation of Millions to
Hold Us Back." But some of the most powerful examples of this art, such as Toni Morrison's masterpiece,
Beloved, bring both tendencies together, creating a new
modality—a sort of lyrical super-naturalism. And that
seems to be the enviable privilege of the new black
artists—today's Post-Mod Squad. In its openness, its
variety, its playfulness with forms, its refusal to follow
a preordained ideological line, its sustained engage-
ments with the black artistic past, today's artistic up-
welling is nourished by the black cultural milieu but
isn't confined by it. "This is a party for those of us who
are comfortable with ambiguity and ambivalence,"
Anna Deavere Smith has remarked. "True art tends to
live there."

THE TALENTED TAR BABY

CERTAINLY it might have been nice to hear a few words about ambiguity and ambivalence when *I* first learned to be black, back when the blaxploitation flicks were first-run, and the draft boards were quite pleased to take college dropouts. *The first time as tragedy; the second time as farce:* for me, the first time wasn't tragedy, quite, but it was as much melodrama as comedy. Still, maybe there are limits even to the ludic. Sometimes the relentless ironicism of contemporary culture feels like a vaccination against earnestness, which is the sort of precaution you take when you've been—in a phrase of Baldwin's—betrayed by too much hoping.

Sometime in my sophomore year, I found myself fighting between becoming the individual I so longingly came to Yale to become and wanting within the deepest part of me to feel black and a vital part of the collective. But wasn't this a game we had played before, when we had baited the white boy? Always before we had won. The game came down to the matter of name. Ralph Ellison describes its workings as follows:

Tar Baby, that enigmatic figure from Negro folklore, stands for the world. He leans, black and gleaming, against the wall of life utterly noncommittal under our scrutiny, our questioning, starkly unmoving before our naive attempts at intimidation. Then we touch him playfully and before we can say *Sonny Liston!* we find ourselves

44

stuck. Our playful investigations become a labor, a fearful struggle, an *agony*. Slowly we perceive that our task is to learn the proper way of freeing ourselves to develop, in other words, technique.

Sensing this, we give him our sharpest attention, we question him carefully, we struggle with more subtlety; while he, in his silent way, holds on, demanding that we perceive the necessity of calling him by his true name as the price of our freedom.

The idea is that we have always had to trick the white man into learning not to take appearances at face value, especially social roles or relationships so tradition-bound as to seem "human" or "natural" or "universal."

I didn't know my college dean very well. It was his first year at Calhoun, as it was mine. I remember with some unease those first few months in the college when, walking as nonchalantly through the courtyard as I was able, I happened too frequently for accident (and frequently enough so that for years later I avoided that route) to cross paths with him. "How's it going," he'd invariably ask, his brow wrinkling with concern. "Do you find our courses difficult? Are you studying enough?" Until the first time he asked, perhaps well into the third week of school, I had pretty much forgotten that I was supposed to feel anxious; I had forgotten the sociological consequences of being black from Appalachia and "at Yale." But I'd try to smile and retort coolly the most relaxed "Yeah" I could manage. And yeah, I was studying every night, all night long. He'd just smile, not having broken stride. Even when I visit today, those walkways reverberate with those "conversations" still.

Amid all the racial and political ferment, I'd decided I wanted to spend a year in Africa (yes, it was an attempt to flee, and maybe even to resolve some of the racial perplexities I'd been experiencing). I went to the dean's office and stated my case as cogently as I could. He smiled benignly, because he understood, then told me how impossible the whole thing was. I think I stopped listening once I heard his tone; for "yes" and "no" are secondary to tone, at least when you find yourself sitting across the desk from some white man whose wallet you're trying to persuade to him share. He wanted to know my name; and I, a Tar Baby, was an arrogant enough part of Yale by now to treasure secretly the knowledge that my college dean didn't know my name. "Hustler" was his first guess; to him, I'd venture, I'm still "hustler" to this day.

For me, it was a matter of getting my bearings. I learned to be black in a world where DeCh and Robby ruled—one infused with the banked outrage and the revolutionary temper of the times. Most of all, I counted myself lucky that I saw DeCh address the May Day rally in 1970, speaking out against the wrongs of Viet Nam and Cambodia, the abuses of the FBI and other nefarious government agencies. He was in his fullest glory that day, as he galvanized a crowd of a hundred thousand with his words and with his very presence. He sizzled; he smote. He was mesmerizing, artfully plaiting mordant humor with passion and uplift, defiance and courage and common sense: he was

Malcolm X and Martin Luther King, Jr., in one. This was DeCh at full strength—a man, as I say, who could lead us into the promised land.

And then? People said he peaked at the May Day rally. Yale was where he'd excelled and Yale was where he would stay, for the longest time. It worried and depressed me that he wouldn't leave New Haven. Years went by, the rest of us dispersed, and he was still in New Haven, where he got a job working in the financial aid office. I think he had dreams—mad, emancipatory dreams—and he needed to wait for those dreams to die. He did leave, finally. One day, he decided to attend law school at the University of Pennsylvania; and he ended up working at the FCC, though he never seemed quite happy there. Whenever we met, over the years, he'd still be chain-smoking his way through a pack and his eyes would sparkle as he repeated stories from the old days—especially the one about how I volunteered to be secretary of the BSAY. And I would smile, and nod, and remember, and sometimes get misty. I was the one he had deputized as his official stenographer, his Boswell. I had seen him at the height of his magnificence, and not only that, I had taken notes.

And sometimes he asked about Robby. Robby, who founded, funded, and ran, superbly, the Carter G. Woodson Institute at the University of Virginia. Robby, who became actively involved in alumni affairs and—it was one of the proudest moments of his life—was awarded the Yale Medal by President A. Bartlett Giamatti. That was one answer you could give to the question about Robby. But there was another answer, too.

Robby, the most brilliant scholar of our set, completed his dissertation with difficulty; and then gave up the ghost. His book? The book, he'd explain, was really two books, he was coming to realize. At least two. He never published the book, though, or anything much at all. Something had more or less stilled his pen for the rest of his professional career. Instead of writing, it seemed, he put on weight.

DeCh died first, less than a year ago. A couple of weeks before, when I learned he was dying of lung cancer, I wrote him a long letter, trying to explain something of what he'd meant to me. Then, a month ago, Robby died: he'd been felled by a stroke, then a heart attack. The weight, the blood pressure, people said—the way middle-aged friends tick off the risk factors, anxious about their own mortality.

Some of the black students I knew at Yale dropped out, or pursued militancy to a point of no return, or went mad: these were still the early days of affirmative action, and this business of recruitment would be considerably refined in the years to come. Jerry was the first to die, stricken, as he was, in the middle of his junior year. Two rumors competed for his epitaph: "overdose," skeptics said; "hemorrhage," replied his friends. There was Tommy, gunned down by Gil Rochon—the tall Am. Stud. grad student from New Orleans who had freckles, a conical Afro, and a wife whom Tommy was sleeping with. There was Eddie Jackson, my roommate, who "broke down" not long after, in hot pursuit of his blackness; later he killed himself by plunging a butcher's knife into his heart.

It is also true that some of the black students I knew

at Yale have gone on to serve in Congress, as big-city mayors, as presidents and vice presidents of major conglomerates. This is what members of the crossover generation are supposed to do: cross over. This is what the civil activists and social engineers who recruited us had in mind. It's how the trope of the "Talented Tenth" was to be retrieved and refashioned for modern times. And yet there's a sense in which DeChabert and Robinson represented more to me than any of the "success stories"; and their failures of fulfillment (the oldest college story of them all) grieved and rankled me as my own. I didn't go to their funerals: the truth is, I wasn't ready for them to be dead, either of them. We were supposed to storm the citadel together, to serve on the Yale Club board of directors together, to summer at Martha's Vineyard together, to grow old together. They would be on hand to explain to me the difference between selling out and buying in. Our kids were supposed to marry each other; to graduate from schools where we would give the commencement addresses. Ours was to be the generation with cultural accountability, and cultural security: the generation that would tell white folks that we would not be deterred—that, whether they knew it or not, we too were of the elite.

But then they had shown me that playing the name game with white folks was relatively easy. It was when we turned the game upon ourselves that the rules became much more subtle. It is a sticky business when two Tar Babies demand to know each other's names. For the names changed from moment to moment; as we discarded one—"the Talented Tenth," say—another would take its place.

The joker, the hole card, was of course that none of us knew our names; we forgot what we called each other when no one else was around. There is something basic to a change of name that is contingent upon illusion, and the very human urge to forget: "negroes" became "Negroes," who in turn became "New Negroes," who much, much later decided to become "Black." Yet through all this, there lurks that marked continuity of social tradition and that sense of the past that informs the imagination. We long to forget, so we change our names: the Talented Tenth?—or a platoon of Uncle Toms? But the discomfort stays the same, and so does the pleasure. As Ralph Ellison said, you gain your invisibility not so much because others refuse to see you but because you refuse to run the gamut of your own humanity. Ultimately, you have no choice; at least I didn't.

As a new recruit, I framed the issue in precisely this manner, allegorical as all get-out. And it was an issue that preoccupied me for some time, one that caused the end of numerous friendships and rendered others impossible even before they had begun. Seeking the refuge of the group after one has been expelled is so much more urgent than that same attempt would have been had we never been members at all. And that black movement of mind, that urge to forget and to start again, afresh, *created* schisms, cemented distinctions among men, far more insidiously than did the increased social mobility of the sixties when white America opened its doors, if ever so slightly. No longer could we be said to be the organic community we seemed to be when King had his day at the Lincoln Memorial.

Scars heal slowly and only partially: Flesh be not proud. You might think of it as a cultural counterpart to the physiological response known as "hyper-pigmentation": the medical fact that black skin responds to injury by getting even blacker. Of course, many of our injuries were self-inflicted.

And even as I was defending myself against those black fellows who had forgotten my name, I found myself struggling to keep white people (even at Yale) from changing my name, taking my name from me. "Black, scholarship boy, remarkable verbal potential for one in his demographic group; mediocre performance. C student." This sort of naming ritual, a self-fulfilling appellative prophecy, they fit interchangeably onto so many of those bright black kids I loved at Yale. So many of us who came to New Haven eager to fulfill that part of ourselves long repressed in ghetto schools and communities far too numerous to name saw our deepest dreams dashed and our deepest fears realized in that sociological naming ritual. If we weren't crushed in a dialectic over what was "black" and what was "blacker," then we were crushed by those bored administrators and jaded teachers who could not see the longing and the impatience to learn buried deep behind the particular mask that each of us chose to wear. Perhaps slipshod, perhaps not so holy, yet these were *our* masks, and the care and the concern and the struggle and joy that went into fashioning and wearing them was all that some of us ever had at Yale and all that some of us have, even now, left of college.

But I was fortunate; I loved the place. I loved the library and the seminars, I loved talking with the professors; I loved "peeping the hole card" in people's assumptions and turning their logic back upon themselves. I had more chip than shoulder, and through it all I demanded of every person with whom I chanced to interact that they earn the right to learn my name. More often than not, white folks stopped at "hustler." And I, like Tar Baby, would tell myself I had won. For years, I would listen for news and watch the mail for word of those I knew there, for news of those I loved and those I despised, of those I trusted and those I feared. Only sometimes do I feel guilty that I was among the lucky ones, and only sometimes do I ask myself why.

BLACK STRIVINGS IN A TWILIGHT CIVILIZATION

CORNEL WEST

*In memory of
my beloved father,
Clifton L. West
(1928–1994)*

How shall Integrity face Oppression? What shall Honesty do in the face of Deception, Decency in the face of Insult, Self-Defense before Blows? How shall Desert and Accomplishment meet Despising, Detraction and Lies? What shall Virtue do to meet Brute Force?
—W. E. B. DU BOIS

The hatred and contempt of the oppressed masses are increasing, and the physical and moral forces of the wealthy are weakening; the deception on which everything depends is wearing out, and the wealthy classes have nothing to console themselves with in this mortal danger.

To return to the old ways is not possible; only one thing is left for those who do not wish to change their way of life, and that is to hope that "things will last my time"—after that let happen what may. That is what the blind crowd of the rich are doing, but the danger is ever growing and the terrible catastrophe draws near.

—LEO TOLSTOY

What we need are books that hit us like a most painful misfortune, like the death of someone we loved more than we love ourselves, that make us feel as though we had been banished to the woods, far from any human presence, like a suicide. A book must be the ax for the frozen sea within us. —FRANZ KAFKA

Speak—
But keep yes and no unsplit.
And give your say this meaning:
Give it the shade.

—PAUL CELAN

W. E. B. Du Bois is the towering black scholar of the twentieth century. The scope of his interests, the depth of his insights, and the sheer majesty of his prolific writings bespeak a level of genius unequaled among modern black intellectuals. Yet, like all of us, Du Bois was a child of his age. He was shaped by the prevailing presuppositions and prejudices of modern Euro-American civilization. And despite his lifelong struggle—marked by great courage and sacrifice—against white supremacy and for the advancement of Africans around the world, he was, in style and substance, a proud black man of letters primarily influenced by nineteenth-century Euro-American traditions.

For those of us interested in the relation of white supremacy to modernity (African slavery in the New World and European imperial domination of most of the rest of the world) or the consequences of the construct of "race" during the Age of Europe (1492–1945), the scholarly and literary works of Du Bois are indispensable. For those of us obsessed with alleviating black social misery, the political texts of Du Bois are insightful and inspiring. In this sense, Du Bois is the brook of fire through which we all must pass in order to gain access to the intellectual and political weaponry needed to sustain the radical democratic tradition in our time.

Yet even this great titan of black emancipation falls short of the mark. This is not to deny the remarkable subtlety of his mind or the undeniable sincerity of his heart. The grand example of Du Bois remains problematic principally owing to his inadequate interpretation of the human condition and his inability to immerse himself fully in the rich cultural currents of black everyday life. His famous notion of the Talented Tenth—including his revised version, articulated in the essay reprinted in the Appendix—reveals this philosophic inadequacy and personal inability.

What does it mean to claim that Du Bois put forward an inadequate interpretation of the human condition or that he failed to immerse himself fully in the cultural depths of black everyday life? Are these simply rhetorical claims devoid of content—too abstract to yield conclusions and too general to evaluate? Are some interpretations of the human condition and cultural ways of life really better than others? If so, why? These crucial questions sit at the center of my critique of Du Bois because they take us to the heart of black life in the profoundly decadent American civilization at the end of the twentieth century—a ghastly century whose levels of barbarity, bestiality, and brutality are unparalleled in human history.

My assessment of Du Bois primarily concerns his response to the problem of evil—to undeserved harm, unjustified suffering, and unmerited pain. Does his evolving worldview, social analysis, and moral vision enable us to understand and endure this "first century of world wars" (Muriel Rukeyser's apt phrase)[1] in which nearly 200 million fellow human beings have been murdered in the name of some pernicious ideology? Does his work contain the necessary intellectual and existential resources enabling us to confront the indescribable agony and unnameable anguish likely to be unleashed in the twenty-first century—the first century involving a systemic gangsterization of everyday life, shot through with revitalized tribalisms—under the aegis of an uncontested, fast-paced global capitalism? As with any great figure, to grapple with Du Bois is to wrestle with who we are, why we are what we are, and what we are to do about it.

Du Bois was first and foremost a black New England Victorian seduced by the Enlightenment ethos and enchanted with the American Dream. His interpretation of the human condition—that is, in part, his idea of who he was and could be—was based on his experiences and, most importantly, on his understanding of those experiences through the medium of an *Enlightenment worldview* that promoted *Victorian strategies* in order to realize an *American optimism;* throughout this essay, I shall probe these three basic foundations of his perspective. Like many of the brilliant and ambitious young men of his time, he breathed the intoxicating fumes of "advanced" intellectual and political culture. Yet in the face of entrenched evil and demonic power, Du Bois often found himself either shipwrecked in the depths of his soul or barely afloat with less and less wind in his existential sails.

My fundamental problem with Du Bois is his inadequate grasp of the tragicomic sense of life—a refusal candidly to confront the sheer absurdity of the human condition. This tragicomic sense—tragicomic rather than simply "tragic," because even ultimate purpose and objective order are called into question—propels us toward suicide or madness unless we are buffered by ritual, cushioned by community, or sustained by art. Du Bois's inability to immerse himself in black everyday life precluded his access to the distinctive black tragicomic sense and black encounter with the absurd. He certainly saw, analyzed, and empathized with black sadness, sorrow, and suffering. But he didn't feel it in his bones deeply enough, nor was he intellectually open enough to position himself alongside the sorrowful, suffering, yet striving ordinary black folk.[2] Instead, his own personal and intellectual distance lifted him above them even as he addressed their plight in his progressive writings. Du Bois was never alienated by black people—he lived in black communities where he received great respect and admiration. But there seemed to be something in him that alienated ordinary black people. In short, he was reluctant to learn fundamental lessons about life—and about himself—from them. Such lessons would have required that he—at least momentarily—believe that they were or might be as wise, insightful, and "advanced" as he; and this he could not do.

Du Bois's Enlightenment worldview—his first foundation—prohibited this kind of understanding. Instead, he adopted a mild elitism that underestimated the capacity of everyday people to "know" about life. In "The Talented Tenth," he claims, "knowledge of life and its wider meaning, has been the point of the Negro's deepest ignorance."[3] In his classic book *The Souls of Black Folk,* there are eighteen references to "black, backward, and ungraceful" folk, including a statement of his intent "to scatter civilization among a people whose ignorance was not simply of letters, but of life itself."[4]

My aim is not to romanticize those whom Sly Stone calls "everyday people" or to cast them as the sole source of wisdom. The myths of the noble savage and the wise commoner are simply the flip sides of the Enlightenment attempts to degrade and devalue everyday people. Yet Du Bois—owing to his Puritan New England origins and Enlightenment values—found it difficult not to view common black folk as some degraded "other" or "alien"—no matter how hard he resisted. His honest response to a church service in the backwoods of Tennessee at a "Southern Negro Revival" bears this out.

A sort of suppressed terror hung in the air and seemed to seize us,—a pythian madness, a demoniac possession, that lent terrible reality to song and word. The black and massive form of the preacher swayed and quivered as the words crowded to his lips and flew at us in singular eloquence. The people moaned and fluttered, and then the gaunt-cheeked brown woman beside me suddenly leaped straight into the air and shrieked like a lost soul, while round about came wail and groan and outcry, and a scene of human passion such as I had never conceived before.

Those who have not thus witnessed the frenzy of a Negro revival in the untouched backwoods of the South can but dimly realize the religious feeling of the slave; as described, such scenes appear grotesque and funny, but as seen they are awful.[5]

Du Bois's intriguing description reminds one of an anthropologist visiting some strange and exotic people whose rituals suggest not only the sublime but also the satanic.[6] The "awfulness" of this black church service, similar to that of my own black Baptist tradition, signifies for him both dread and fear, anxiety and disgust. In short, a black ritualistic explosion of energy frightened this black rationalist. It did so not simply because the folk seem so coarse and uncouth, but also because they are out of control, overpowered by something bigger than themselves. This clearly posed a threat to him.

Like a good Enlightenment *philosophe,* Du Bois pits autonomy against authority, self-mastery against tradition. Autonomy and self-mastery connote self-consciousness and self-criticism; authority and tradition suggest blind deference and subordination. Self-consciousness and self-criticism yield cosmopolitanism and highbrow culture. Authority and tradition reinforce provincialism and lowbrow culture. The educated and chattering class—the Talented Tenth—are the agents of sophistication and mastery, while the uneducated and moaning class—the backward masses—remain locked in tradition; the basic role of the Talented Tenth is to civilize and refine, uplift and elevate the benighted masses.[7]

For Du Bois, education was the key. Ignorance was the major obstacle—black ignorance and white ignorance. If the black masses were educated—in order to acquire skills and culture—black America would thrive. If white elites and masses were enlightened, they would not hate and fear black folk. Hence America—black and white—could be true to its democratic ideals.

The Negro Problem was in my mind a matter of systematic investigation and intelligent understanding. The world was thinking wrong about race, because it did not know. The ultimate evil was stupidity. The cure for it was knowledge based on scientific investigation.[8]

This Enlightenment naïveté—not only in regard to white supremacy but with respect to any form of personal and institutional evil—was momentarily shaken by a particular case involving that most peculiar American institution—lynching.

At the very time when my studies were most successful, there cut across this plan which I had as a scientist, a red ray which could not be ignored. I remember when it first, as it were, startled me to my feet: a poor Negro in central Georgia, Sam Hose, had killed his landlord's wife. I wrote out a careful and reasoned statement concerning the evident facts and started down to the Atlanta Constitution office. . . . I did not get there. On the way news met me: Sam Hose had been lynched, and they said that his knuckles were on exhibition at a grocery store farther down on Mitchell Street, along which I was walking. I turned back to the university. I began to turn aside from my work. . . .

Two considerations thereafter broke in upon my work and eventually disrupted it: first, one could not be a calm, cool, and detached scientist while Negroes were lynched, murdered and starved; and secondly, there was no such definite demand for scientific work of the sort that I was doing. . . .[9]

Then, in the very next month, Du Bois lost his eighteen-month-old son, Burghardt, to diphtheria.[10] If ever Du Bois was forced to confront the tragedy of life and the absurdity of existence, it was in the aftermath of this loss, which he describes in his most moving piece of writing, "Of the Passing of the First-Born" in *The Souls of Black Folk*. In this powerful elegiac essay, Du Bois not only mourns his son but speaks directly to death itself—as Prometheus to Zeus or Jesus to his Heavenly Father.[11]

But hearken, O Death! Is not this my life hard enough,—is not that dull land that stretches its sneering web about me cold enough,—is not all the world beyond these four little walls pitiless enough, but that thou must needs enter here,— thou, O Death? About my head the thundering storm beat like a heartless voice, and the crazy forest pulsed with the curses of the weak; but what cared I, within my home beside my wife and baby boy? Wast thou so jealous of one little coign of happiness that thou must needs enter there,— thou, O Death?[12]

This existential gall to go face-to-face and toe-to-toe with death in order to muster some hope against hope is echoed in his most tragic characterization of the black sojourn in white supremacist America.

Within the Veil was he born, said I; and there within shall he live,—a Negro and a Negro's son. Holding in that little head—ah, bitterly!—the un-bowed pride of a hunted race, clinging with that tiny dimpled hand—ah, wearily!—to a hope not hopeless but unhopeful, and seeing with those bright wondering eyes that peer into my soul a land whose freedom is to us a mockery and whose liberty a lie.[13]

What is most revealing in this most poignant of mo-ments is Du Bois's refusal to linger with the sheer tragedy of his son's death (a natural, not a social, evil)—without casting his son as an emblem of the race or a symbol of a black deliverance to come.[14] Despite the deep sadness in this beautiful piece of writing, Du Bois sidesteps Dostoyevsky's challenge to wrestle in a sustained way with the irrevocable fact of an innocent child's death. Du Bois's rationalism prevents him from wading in such frightening existential waters. Instead, Du Bois rushes to glib theodicy, weak allegory, and su-perficial symbolism (see pages 183–84 for a further ar-gument regarding this fascinating text). In other words, his Enlightenment worldview falters in the face of death—the deaths of Sam Hose and Burghardt. The deep despair that lurks around the corner is held at arm's length by rational attempts to boost his flagging spirit.

Du Bois's principal intellectual response to the limits of his Enlightenment worldview was to incorporate certain insights of Marx and Freud. Yet Marx's power-ful critique of the unequal relations of power between capitalists and the proletariat in the workplace and Freud's penetrating attempt to exercise rational control over the irrational forces at work in self and society only deepened Du Bois's commitment to the Enlightenment ethos. And though particular features of this ethos are essential to any kind of intellectual integrity and democratic vision—features such as self-criticism and self-development, suspicion of illegitimate authority and suffocating tradition—the Enlightenment worldview held by Du Bois is ultimately inadequate, and, in many ways, antiquated, for our time. The tragic plight and absurd predicament of Africans here and abroad requires a more profound interpretation of the human condition—one that goes far beyond the false dichotomies of expert knowledge vs. mass ignorance, individual autonomy vs. dogmatic authority, and self-mastery vs. intolerant tradition. Our tragicomic times require more democratic concepts of knowledge and leadership which highlight human fallibility and mutual accountability; notions of individuality and contested authority which stress dynamic traditions; and ideals of self-realization within participatory communities.

The second fundamental pillar of Du Bois's intellectual project is his Victorian strategies—namely, the ways in which his Enlightenment worldview can be translated into action. They rest upon three basic assumptions. First, that the self-appointed agents of Enlightenment constitute a sacrificial cultural elite engaged in service on behalf of the impulsive and irrational masses. Second, that this service consists of shaping and molding the values and viewpoints of the

masses by managing educational and political bureaucracies (e.g., schools and political parties). Third, that
the effective management of these bureaucracies by the
educated few for the benefit of the pathetic many pro-
motes material and spiritual progress. These assumptions form the terrain upon which the Talented Tenth
are to operate.

In fact, Du Bois's notion of the Talented Tenth is a
descendant of those cultural and political elites conceived by the major Victorian critics during the heyday
of the British Empire in its industrial phase.[15] S. T.
Coleridge's secular clerisy, Thomas Carlyle's strong
heroes, and Matthew Arnold's disinterested aliens all
shun the superficial vulgarity of materialism and the
cheap thrills of hedonism in order to preserve and promote highbrow culture and to civilize and contain the
lowbrow masses. The resounding first and last sen-
tences of Du Bois's essay "The Talented Tenth" not
only echo the "truths" of Victorian social criticism,
they also bestow upon the educated few a salvific role.
"The Negro race, like all races, is going to be saved by
its exceptional men."[16] This bold statement is descrip-
tive, prescriptive, and predictive. It assumes that the
exceptional men of other races have saved their "race"
(Gladstone in Britain, Menelik in Ethiopia, Bismarck
in Germany, Napoleon in France, Peter in Russia?).
Here Du Bois claims that exceptional black men ought
to save their "race" and asserts that if any "race"—
especially black people—is to be saved, exceptional
men will do it. The patriarchal sensibilities speak for
themselves.[17]

Like a good Victorian critic, Du Bois argues on rational grounds for the legitimacy of his cultural elite. They are worthy of leadership because they are educated and trained, refined and civilized, disciplined and determined. Most important, they have "honesty of heart" and "purity of motive." Contrast Matthew Arnold's disinterested aliens, "who are mainly led, not by their class spirit, but by a general *humane* spirit, by the love of human perfection," in *Culture and Anarchy* (1869) with Du Bois's Talented Tenth.

The men of culture are the true apostles of equality. The great men of culture are those who have had a passion for diffusing, for making prevail, for carrying from one end of society to the other, the best knowledge, the best ideas of their time, who have laboured to divest knowledge of all that was harsh, uncouth, difficult, abstract, professional, exclusive; to humanize it, to make it efficient outside the clique of the cultivated and learned, yet still remaining the *best* knowledge and thought of the time, and a true source, therefore, of sweetness and light.[18]

Who are to-day guiding the work of the Negro people? The "exceptions" of course. . . . A saving remnant continually survives and persists, continually aspires, continually shows itself in thrift and ability and character. . . .

Can the masses of the Negro people be in any possible way more quickly raised than by the effort and example of this aristocracy of talent and character? Was there ever a nation on God's fair earth civilized from the bottom upward? Never; it is, ever was and ever will be from the top downward that culture filters. The Talented Tenth rises and pulls all that are worth the saving up to their vantage ground. This is the history of human progress; and the two historic mistakes which have hindered that progress were the thinking first that no more could ever rise save the few already risen; or second, that it would better the unrisen to pull the risen down.[19]

Just as Arnold seeks to carve out discursive space and a political mission for the educated elite in the British Empire somewhere between the arrogance and complacency of the aristocracy and the vulgarity and anarchy of the working classes, Du Bois wants to create a new vocabulary and social vocation for the black educated elite in America somewhere between the hatred and scorn of the white supremacist majority and the crudity and illiteracy of the black agrarian masses. Yet his gallant efforts suffer from intellectual defects and historical misconceptions.

Let us begin with the latter. Is it true that in 1903 the educated elite were guiding the work of the Negro people? Yes and no. Certainly the most visible national black leaders tended to be educated black men, such as the ubiquitous Booker T. Washington and, of course, Du Bois himself. Yet the two most effective political forms of organizing and mobilizing among black people were the black women's club movement led by Ida B. Wells and the migration movement guided by Benjamin "Pap" Singleton, A. A. Bradley, and Richard H.

Cain.[20] Both movements were based in black civil society—that is, black civic associations like churches, lodges, fraternal orders, and sororities. Their fundamental goals were neither civil rights nor social equality but rather respect and dignity, land and self-determination. How astonishing—and limiting—that Du Bois fails to mention and analyze these movements that will result in the great Mary McLeod Bethune's educational crusade and the inimitable Marcus Garvey's Back-to-Africa movement in a decade or so!

Regarding the intellectual defects of Du Bois's noble endeavor: first, he assumes that highbrow culture is inherently humanizing, and that exposure to and immersion in great works produce good people. Yet we have little reason to believe that people who delight in the works of geniuses like Mozart and Beethoven or Goethe and Wordsworth are any more or less humane than those who dance in the barnyards to the banjo plucking of nameless rural folk in Tennessee. Certainly those fervent white supremacists who worship the Greek and Roman classics and revel in the plays of the incomparable Shakespeare weaken his case.[21] Second, Du Bois holds that the educated elite can more easily transcend their individual and class interests and more readily act on behalf of the common good than the uneducated masses. But is this so? Are they not just as prone to corruption and graft, envy and jealousy, self-destructive passion and ruthless ambition as everyone else? Were not Carlyle's great heroes, Cromwell and Napoleon, tyrants? Was it not Arnold's disinterested aliens who promoted and implemented the inhumane policies of the imperial British bureaucracies in India and Africa? Was not Du Bois himself both villain and victim in petty political games as well as in the all-too-familiar social exclusions of the educated elite?

Du Bois wisely acknowledges this problem in his 1948 revision of "The Talented Tenth":

> When I came out of college into the world of work, I realized that it was quite possible that my plan of training a talented tenth might put in control and power, a group of selfish, self-indulgent, well-to-do men, whose basic interest in solving the Negro Problem was personal; personal freedom and unhampered enjoyment and use of the world, without any real care, or certainly no arousing care, as to what became of the mass of American Negroes, or of the mass of any people. My Talented Tenth, I could see, might result in a sort of interracial free-for-all, with the devil taking the hindmost and the foremost taking anything they could lay hands on.[22]

He then notes the influence of Marx on his thinking and adds that the Talented Tenth must not only be talented but have "expert knowledge" of modern economics, be willing to sacrifice and plan effectively to institute socialist measures. Yet there is still no emphatic call for accountability from below, nor any grappling with the evil that lurks in the hearts of all of us. He recognizes human selfishness as a problem without putting forward adequate philosophical responses to it or institutional mechanisms to alleviate it. In the end, he throws up his hands and gives us a grand either/or option. "But we must have honest men or we die. We must have unselfish, far-seeing leadership or we fail."[23]

Victorian social criticism contains elements indispensable to future critical thought about freedom and democracy in the twenty-first century. Most important, it elevates the role of public intellectuals who put forward overarching visions and broad analyses based on a keen sense of history and a subtle grasp of the way the world is going in the present. The rich tradition of Victorian critics—Thomas Carlyle, John Ruskin, Matthew Arnold, John Morley, William Morris, and, in our own century, L. T. Hobhouse, J. A. Hobson, C. F. G. Masterman, R. H. Tawney, Raymond Williams, E. P. Thompson, and others—stands shoulders above the parochial professionalism of much of the academy today. In our era, scholarship is often divorced from public engagement, and shoddy journalism often settles for the sensational and superficial aspects of prevailing crises.[24] As the distinguished European man of letters George Steiner notes in regard to the academy,

Specialization has reached moronic vehemence. Learned lives are expended on reiterative minutiae. Academic rewards go to the narrow scholiast, to the blinkered. Men and women in the learned professions proclaim themselves experts on one author, in one brief historical period, in one aesthetic medium. They look with contempt (and dank worry) on the "Generalist." ... It may be that cows have fields. The geography of consciousness should be that of unfenced *errance,* Montaigne's comely word.[25]

Yet the Victorian strategies of Du Bois require not piecemeal revision but wholesale reconstruction. A fuller understanding of the human condition should lead us far beyond any notions of free-floating elites, suspicious of the tainted masses—elites who worship at the altar of highbrow culture while ignoring the barbarity and bestiality in their own ranks. The fundamental role of the public intellectual—distinct from, yet building on, the indispensable work of academics, experts, analysts, and pundits—is to create and sustain high-quality public discourse addressing urgent public problems which enlightens and energizes fellow citizens, prompting them to take public action. This role requires a deep commitment to the life of the mind—a perennial attempt to clear our minds of cant (to use Samuel Johnson's famous formulation)—which serves to shape the public destiny of a people. Intellectual and political leadership is neither elitist nor populist; rather it is democratic, in that each of us stands in public space, without humiliation, to put forward our best visions and views for the sake of the public interest. And these arguments are presented in an atmosphere of mutual respect and civic trust.

The last pillar of Du Bois's project is his American optimism. Like most intellectuals of the New World, he was preoccupied with progress. And given his genuine commitment to black advancement, this preoccupation is understandable. Yet, writing as he was in the early stages of the consolidation of the American Empire (some eight million people of color had been incorporated after the Spanish-American War), when the U.S. itself was undergoing geographical and economic expansion and millions of "new" Americans were being admitted from eastern Europe, Du Bois tended to assume that U.S. expansionism was a sign of probable American progress. In this sense, in his early and middle years, he was not only a progressivist but also a kind of American exceptionalist.[26] It must be said, to be sure, that unlike most American exceptionalists of his day, he considered the color line the major litmus test for the country. Yet he remained optimistic about a multiracial democratic America.

Du Bois never fully grasped the deeply pessimistic view of American democracy behind the Garvey movement.[27] In fact, he never fully understood or appreciated the strong—though not central—black nationalist strain in the Black Freedom movement. As much as he hated white supremacy in America, he could never bring himself to identify intimately with the harsh words of the great performing artist Josephine Baker, who noted in response to the East St. Louis Riot of July 1917 that left over two hundred black people dead and over six thousand homeless, "The very idea of America makes me shake and tremble and gives me nightmares." Baker lived most of her life in exile in France. Even when Du Bois left for Africa in 1961—as a member of a moribund Communist Party—his attitude toward America was not that of an Elijah Muhammad or a Malcolm X. He was still, in a significant sense, disappointed with America, and there is no disappointment without some dream deferred. Elijah Muhammad and Malcolm X were not disappointed with America. As bona fide black nationalists, they had no expectations of a white supremacist civilization; they adhered neither to American optimism nor to exceptionalism.

Black nationalism is a complex tradition of thought and action, a tradition best expressed in the numerous insightful texts of black public intellectuals like Maulana Karenga, Imamu Amiri Baraka, Haki R. Madhubuti, Marimba Ani, and Molefi Asante. Black nationalists usually call upon black people to close ranks, to distrust most whites (since the reliable whites are few and relatively powerless in the face of white supremacy), and to promote forms of black self-love, self-defense, and self-determination. It views white supremacy as the definitive systemic constraint on black cultural, political, and economic development. More pointedly, black nationalists claim that American democracy is a modern form of tyranny on the part of the white majority over the black minority. For them, black sanity and freedom requires that America not serve as the major framework in which to understand the future of black people. Instead, American civilization—like all civilizations—rises and falls, ebbs and flows. And owing to its deep-seated racism, this society does not warrant black allegiance or loyalty. White supremacy dictates the limits of the operation of American democracy—with black folk the indispensable sacrificial lamb vital to its sustenance. Hence black subordination constitutes the necessary condition for the flourishing of American democracy, the tragic prerequisite for America itself. This is, in part, what

Richard Wright meant when he noted, "The Negro is America's metaphor."

The most courageous and consistent of twentieth-century black nationalists—Marcus Garvey and Elijah Muhammad—adamantly rejected any form of American optimism or exceptionalism. Du Bois feared that if they were right, he would be left in a state of paralyzing despair. A kind of despair that results not only when all credible options for black freedom in America are closed, but also when the very framework needed to understand and cope with that despair is shattered. The black nationalist challenge to Du Bois cuts much deeper than the rational and political possibilities for change—it resides at the visceral and existential levels of what to do about "what is" or when "what ought to be done" seems undoable. This frightening sense of foreboding pervades much of black America today—a sense that fans and fuels black nationalism.

Du Bois's American optimism screened him from this dark night of the soul. His American exceptionalism guarded him from that gray twilight between "nothing to be done" and "I can't go on like this"—a Beckett-like dilemma in which the wait and search for Godot, or for freedom, seem endless. This militant despair about the black condition is expressed in that most arresting of black nationalist speeches by Rev. Henry Highland Garnet in 1843:

If we must bleed, let it come all at once—rather die freemen than live to be slaves. It is impossible like the children of Israel, to make a grand Exodus from the land of bondage. The pharaoh's on both sides of the blood-red waters![28]

Du Bois's response to such despair is to say "we surely must do something"—for such rebellion is suicidal and the notion of a separate black nation quixotic. So, he seems to say, let us continue to wait and search for Godot in America—even if it seems, with our luck, that all we get is "Pozzo" (new forms of disrespect, disregard, degradation, and defamation).

American optimism couched within the ideals of the American experiment contains crucial components for any desirable form of black self-determination or modern nationhood: precious standards of constitutional democracy, the rule of law, individual liberties, and the dignity of common folk. Yet American optimism—in the ugly face of American white supremacist practices—warrants, if not outright rejection, at least vast attenuation. The twenty-first century will almost certainly not be a time in which American exceptionalism will flower in the world or American optimism will flourish among people of African descent.

If there are any historical parallels between black Americans at the end of the twentieth century and other peoples in earlier times, two candidates loom large: Tolstoy's Russia and Kafka's Prague—soul-starved Russians a generation after the emancipation of the serfs in 1861 and anxiety-ridden Central European Jews a generation before the European Holocaust in the 1940s. Indeed, my major intellectual disappointment with the great Du Bois lies in the fact that there are hardly any traces in his work of any serious grappling with the profound thinkers and spiritual wrestlers in the modern West from these two groups—major figures obsessed with the problem of evil in their time.

We see in Du Bois no engagement with Leo Tolstoy, Fyodor Dostoyevsky, Ivan Turgenev, Alexander Herzen, Lev Shestov, Anton Chekhov, or Franz Kafka, Max Brod, Kurt Tucholsky, Hermann Broch, Hugo Bergmann, or Karl Kraus. These omissions are glaring because the towering figures in both groups were struggling with political and existential issues similar to those facing black people in America. For example, the Russian situation involved the humanity of degraded impoverished peasants, the fragile stability of an identity-seeking empire, and the alienation of superfluous intellectuals; the Central European Jewish circumstance, the humanity of devalued middle-class Jews, the imminent collapse of a decadent empire, and the militant despair of self-hating intellectuals. The intellectual response on the part of the Russian authors was what Hegel would call "world-historical"—they wrote many of the world's greatest novels, short stories, essays, and plays. The writers I cite put forward profound interpretations of the human condition which rejected any Enlightenment worldview, Victorian strategy, or worldly optimism. And although the Central European Jewish authors are often overlooked by contemporary intellectuals—owing to a tendency to focus on Western Europe—their intellectual response was monumental. They composed many of this century's most probing and penetrating novels, short stories, autobiographies, and letters.

Both Russian and Central European Jewish writers share deep elective affinities that underlie their distinctive voices: the "wind of the wing of madness" (to use Baudelaire's phrase) beats incessantly on their souls. The fear of impending social doom and dread of inevitable death haunt them, and they search for a precious individuality in the face of a terror-ridden society and a seductive (yet doubtful) nationalist option.[29] In short, fruitful comparisons may be made between the Russian sense of the tragic and the Central European Jewish sense of the absurd and the black intellectual response to the African-American predicament. Tolstoy's *War and Peace* (1869), *The Death of Ivan Ilych* (1886), and "How Much Land Does a Man Need?" (1886) and Chekhov's *The Three Sisters* (1901)—the greatest novel, short story, brief tale, and play in modern Europe—and Kafka's "The Judgment" (1913), "The Metamorphosis" (1915), and "In the Penal Colony" (1919) and "The Burrow"(1923)—some of the grandest fictive portraits of twentieth-century Europe—constitute the highest moments and most ominous murmurings in Europe before it entered the ugly and fiery inferno of totalitarianism. Similarly, the intellectual response of highbrow black artists—most of whom are musicians and often of plebeian origins—probe the depths of a black sense of the tragic and absurd which yields a subversive joy and sublime melancholia unknown to most in the New World. The form and content of Louis Armstrong's "West End Blues," Duke Ellington's "Mood Indigo," John Coltrane's "Alabama," and Sarah Vaughan's "Send in the Clowns" are a few of the peaks of the black cultural iceberg—towering examples of soul-making and spiritual wrestling which crystallize the most powerful interpretations of the human condition in black life. This is why the best of the black musical tradition in the twentieth century is the most profound and poignant body of artistic works in our time.

Like their Russian and Central European Jewish counterparts, the black artists grapple with madness and melancholia, doom and death, terror and horror, individuality and identity. Unlike them, the black artists do so against the background of an African heritage that puts a premium on voice and body, sound and silence, and the foreground is occupied by an American tradition that highlights mobility and novelty, individuality and democracy. The explosive products of this multilayered cultural hybridity—with its new diasporic notions of time and space, place and face—take us far beyond Du Bois's enlightened optimism. Instead, the profound black cultural efforts to express the truth of modern tragic existence and build on the ruins of modern absurd experiences at the core of American culture take us to the end of this dreadful century. These black artistic endeavors prefigure and pose the most fundamental and formidable challenges to a twilight civilization—an American Empire adrift on turbulent seas in a dark fog. William Faulkner, Mark Twain, Thomas Pynchon, and, above all, the incomparable Herman Melville—the only great Euro-American novelists to be spoken of in the same breath as Tolstoy and Kafka, Armstrong and Coltrane—grasp crucial aspects of this black condition. Just as Richard Wright, Ralph Ellison, James Baldwin, and, preeminently, Toni Morrison guide us through the tragedies and absurdities within the Veil (or behind the color curtain) to disclose on the page what is best revealed in black song, speech, sermon, bodily performance, and the eloquence of black silence. Yet despite his shortcomings, the great Du Bois remains the springboard for any examination of black strivings in American civilization.

ON BLACK STRIVINGS

BLACK STRIVINGS are the creative and complex products of the terrifying African encounter with the absurd *in* America—and the absurd *as* America. Like any other group of human beings, black people forged ways of life and ways of struggle under circumstances not of their own choosing. They constructed structures of meaning and structures of feeling in the face of the fundamental facts of human existence—death, dread, despair, disease, and disappointment. Yet the specificity of black culture—namely, those features that distinguish black culture from other cultures—lies in both the *African* and *American* character of black people's attempts to sustain their mental sanity and spiritual health, social life and political struggle in the midst of a slaveholding, white supremacist civilization that viewed itself as the most enlightened, free, tolerant, and democratic experiment in human history.

Any serious examination of black culture should begin with what W. E. B. Du Bois dubbed, in Faustian terms, the "spiritual strivings" of black people—the dogged determination to survive and subsist, the tenacious will to persevere, persist, and maybe even prevail.[30] These "strivings" occur within the whirlwind of white supremacy—that is, as responses to the vicious attacks on black beauty, black intelligence, black moral character, black capability, and black possibility. To put it bluntly, every major institution in American society—churches, universities, courts, academies of science, governments, economies, newspapers, magazines, television, film, and others—attempted to exclude black people from the human family in the name of white supremacist ideology. This unrelenting assault on black humanity produced the fundamental condition of black culture—that of *black invisibility and namelessness.*

This basic predicament exists on at least four levels—existential, social, political, and economic. The existential level is the most relevant here because it has to do with what it means to be a person and live a life under the horrifying realities of racist assault. To be a black human being under circumstances in which one's humanity is questioned is not only to face a difficult challenge but also to exercise a demanding discipline.

The sheer absurdity of being a black human being whose black body is viewed as an abomination, whose black thoughts and ideas are perceived as debased, and whose black pain and grief are rendered invisible on the human and moral scale is the New World context in which black culture emerged. Black people are first and foremost an African people, in that the cultural baggage they brought with them to the New World was grounded in their earlier responses to African conditions. Yet the rich African traditions—including the kinetic orality, passionate physicality, improvisational intellectuality, and combative spirituality—would undergo creative transformation when brought into contact with European languages and rituals in the context of the New World. For example, there would be no jazz without New World Africans with European languages and instruments.

On the crucial existential level relating to black invisibility and namelessness, the first difficult challenge and demanding discipline is to ward off madness and discredit suicide as a desirable option. A central preoccupation of black culture is that of confronting candidly the ontological wounds, psychic scars, and existential bruises of black people while fending off insanity and self-annihilation. Black culture consists of black modes of being-in-the-world obsessed with black sadness and sorrow, black agony and anguish, black heartache and heartbreak without fully succumbing to the numbing effects of such misery—to never allow such misery to have the last word. This is why the "urtext" of black culture is neither a word nor a book, not an architectural monument or a legal brief. Instead, it is a guttural cry and a wrenching moan—a cry not so much for help as for home, a moan less out of complaint than for recognition. The most profound black cultural products—John Coltrane's saxophone solos, James Cleveland's gut gospels, Billie Holiday's vocal leaps, Rev. Gardner Taylor's rhapsodic sermons, James Baldwin's poignant essays, Alvin Ailey's graceful dances, Toni Morrison's dissonant novels—transform and transfigure in artistic form this cry and moan. The deep black meaning of this cry and moan goes back to the indescribable cries of Africans on the slave ships during the cruel transatlantic voyages to America and the indecipherable moans of enslaved Afro-Americans on Wednesday nights or Sunday mornings near god-forsaken creeks or on wooden benches at prayer meetings in makeshift black churches. This fragile existential arsenal—rooted in silent tears and weary lament—supports black endurance against madness and suicide. The primal black cries and moans lay bare the profoundly tragicomic character of black life. Ironically, they also embody the life-preserving content of black styles—creative ways of fashioning power and strength through the body and language which yield black joy and ecstasy.

Du Bois captures one such primal scene of black culture at the beginning of *The Souls of Black Folk* (1903), in chapter 1, "Of Our Spiritual Strivings." He starts with thirteen lines from the poem "The Crying of Water" by Arthur Symons, the English symbolist critic and decadent poet who went mad a few years after writing the poem. The hearts of human beings in a heartless slave trade cry out like the sea: "All life long crying without avail, / As the water all night long is crying to me."[31]

This metaphorical association of black hearts, black people, and black culture with water (the sea or a river) runs deep in black artistic expression—as in Langston Hughes's recurring refrain, "My soul has grown deep like the rivers," in "The Negro Speaks of Rivers." Black striving resides primarily in movement and motion, resilience and resistance against the paralysis of madness and the stillness of death. As it is for Jim in Mark Twain's *The Adventures of Huckleberry Finn* (1885), the river—a road that moves—is the means by which black people can flee from a menacing racist society.

Du Bois continues with the musical bars of the Negro spiritual "Nobody Knows the Trouble I've Seen." This spiritual is known not simply for its plaintive melody but also for its inexplicable lyrical reversal.

> *Nobody knows the trouble I've seen*
> *Nobody knows but Jesus*
> *Nobody knows the trouble I've seen*
> *Glory hallelujah!*[32]

This exemplary shift from a mournful brooding to a joyful praising is the product of courageous efforts to look life's abyss in the face and keep "keepin' on." This struggle is sustained primarily by the integrity of style, song, and spirituality in a beloved community (e.g., Jesus' proclamation of the Kingdom). It is rather like Ishmael's tragicomic "free and easy sort of genial, desperado philosophy" in *Moby-Dick,* but it is intensified by the fiery art of Aretha Franklin's majestic shouts for joy.

The first of Du Bois's own words in the text completes the primal scene of black culture:

Between me and the other world there is ever an unasked question: unasked by some through feelings of delicacy; by others through the difficulty of rightly framing it. All, nevertheless, flutter round it. They approach me in a half-hesitant sort of way, eye me curiously or compassionately, and then, instead of saying directly, How does it feel to be a problem? they say, I know an excellent colored man in my town; or, I fought at Mechanicsville; or, Do not these Southern outrages make your blood boil? At these I smile, or am interested, or reduce the boiling to a simmer, as the occasion may require. To the real question, How does it feel to be a problem? I answer seldom a word.

And yet, being a problem is a strange experience,—peculiar even for one who has never been anything else, save perhaps in babyhood. . . .[33]

This seminal passage spells out the basic components of black invisibility and namelessness: *black people as a problem-people rather than people with problems; black people as abstractions and objects rather than individuals and persons; black and white worlds divided by a thick wall (or a "Veil") that requires role-playing and mask-wearing rather than genuine humane interaction; black rage, anger, and fury concealed in order to assuage white fear and anxiety; and black people rootless and homeless on a perennial journey to discover who they are in a society content to see blacks remain the permanent underdog.*

To view black people as a problem-people is to view them as an undifferentiated blob, a homogeneous bloc, or a monolithic conglomerate. Each black person is interchangeable, indistinguishable, or substitutable since all black people are believed to have the same views and values, sentiments and sensibilities. Hence one set of negative stereotypes holds for all of them, no matter how high certain blacks may ascend in the white world (e.g., "savages in a suit or suite"). And the mere presence of black bodies in a white context generates white unease and discomfort, even among whites of goodwill.

This problematizing of black humanity deprives black people of individuality, diversity, and heterogeneity. It reduces black folk to abstractions and objects born of white fantasies and insecurities—as exotic or transgressive entities, as hypersexual or criminal animals.[34] The celebrated opening passage of Ralph Ellison's classic novel, *Invisible Man* (1952), highlights this reduction.

> I am an invisible man. No, I am not a spook like those who haunted Edgar Allan Poe; nor am I one of your Hollywood-movie ectoplasms. I am a man of substance, of flesh and bone, fiber and liquids—and I might even be said to possess a mind. I am invisible, understand, simply because people refuse to see me. Like the bodiless heads you see sometimes in circus sideshows, it is as though I have been surrounded by mirrors of hard, distorting glass. When they approach me they see only my surroundings, themselves, or figments of their imagination—indeed, everything and anything except me.[35]

This distorted perception—the failure to see the humanity and individuality of black people—has its source in the historic "Veil" (slavery, Jim Crow, and segregation) that separates the black and white worlds. Ironically, this refusal to see a people whose epidermis is most visible exists alongside a need to keep tight surveillance over these people. This Veil not only precludes honest communication between blacks and whites; it also forces blacks to live in two worlds in order to survive. Whites need not understand or live in the black world in order to thrive. But blacks must grapple with the painful "double-consciousness" that may result in "an almost morbid sense of personality and a moral hesitancy which is fatal to self-confidence."[36] Du Bois notes,

> The worlds within and without the Veil of Color are changing, and changing rapidly, but not at the same rate, not in the same way; and this must produce a peculiar wrenching of the soul, a peculiar sense of doubt and bewilderment. Such a double life, with double thoughts, double duties, and double social classes, must give rise to double words and double ideals, and tempt the mind to pretence or to revolt, to hypocrisy or to radicalism.[37]

Echoing Paul Laurence Dunbar's famous poem "We Wear the Mask," Du Bois proclaims that "the price of culture is a Lie."[38] Why? Because black people will not succeed in American society if they are fully and freely themselves. Instead, they must "endure petty insults with a smile, shut [their] eyes to wrong."[39] They must not be too frank and outspoken and must never fail to flatter and be pleasant in order to lessen white unease and discomfort. Needless to say, this is not the raw stuff for healthy relations between black and white people.

Yet this suppression of black rage—the reducing "the boiling to a simmer"—backfires in the end. It reinforces a black obsession with the psychic scars, ontological wounds, and existential bruises that tend to reduce the tragic to the pathetic. Instead of exercising agency or engaging in action against the odds, one may wallow in self-pity, acknowledging the sheer absurdity of it all. After playing the role and wearing the mask in the white world, one may accept the white world's view of one's self. As Du Bois writes,

> It is a peculiar sensation, this double-consciousness, this sense of always looking at one's self through the eyes of others, of measuring one's soul by the tape of a world that looks on in amused contempt and pity.[40]

Toni Morrison explores this dilemma of black culture through her moving portrayal of the character of Sweet Home in her profound novel *Beloved* (1987), similar to Jean Toomer's Karintha and Fern in his marvelous and magical text *Cane* (1923).

> For the sadness was at her center, the desolated center where the self that was no self made its home.[41]

This theme of black rootlessness and homelessness is inseparable from black namelessness. When James

Baldwin writes about these issues in *Nobody Knows My Name* (1961) and *No Name in the Street* (1972), he is trying to explore effective ways to resist the white supremacist imposition of subordinate roles, stations, and identities on blacks. He is attempting to devise some set of existential strategies against the overwhelming onslaught of white dehumanization, devaluation, and degradation. The search for black space (home), black place (roots), and black face (name) is a flight from the visceral effects of white supremacy. Toni Morrison characterizes these efforts as products of a process of "dirtying you."

> That anybody white could take your whole self for anything that came to mind. Not just work, kill, or maim you, but dirty you. Dirty you so bad you couldn't like yourself anymore. Dirty you so bad you forgot who you were and couldn't think it up.[42]

Toni Morrison's monumental novel holds a privileged place in black culture and modernity precisely because she takes this dilemma to its logical conclusion—that black flight from white supremacy (a chamber of horrors for black people) may lead to the murder of those loved ones who are candidates for the "dirtying" process. The black mother, Sethe, kills her daughter, Beloved, because she loved her so, "to out-hurt the hurter," as an act of resistance against the "dirtying" process.

And though she and others lived through and got over it, she could never let it happen to her own. The best thing she was, was her children. Whites might dirty *her* all right, but not her best thing, her beautiful, magical best thing—the part of her that was clean. No undreamable dreams about whether the headless, feetless torso hanging in the tree with a sign on it was her husband or Paul A; whether the bubbling-hot girls in the colored-school fire set by patriots included her daughter; whether a gang of whites invaded her daughter's private parts, soiled her daughter's thighs and threw her daughter out of the wagon. *She* might have to work the slaughterhouse yard, but not her daughter.

And no one, nobody on this earth, would list her daughter's characteristics on the animal side of the paper. No. Oh no. . . . Sethe had refused—and refused still.

. . . [W]hat she had done was right because it came from true love.[43]

Is death the only black space (home), place (roots), and face (name) safe from a pervasive white supremacy? Toni Morrison's Sethe echoes Du Bois's own voice upon the painful passing of his first-born. For Sethe, as for Tolstoy's Ivan, Chekhov's Bishop Pyotr, Kafka's Josephine, Hawthorne's Goodman Brown, Hardy's Jude, Büchner's Woyzeck, Dreiser's Hurstwood, and Shakespeare's Lear, death is the great liberator from suffering and evil.

But Love sat beside his cradle, and in his ear Wisdom waited to speak. Perhaps now he knows the All-love, and needs not to be wise. Sleep, then, child,—sleep till I sleep and waken to a baby voice and the ceaseless patter of little feet—above the Veil.[44]

The most effective and enduring black responses to invisibility and namelessness are those forms of individual and collective black resistance predicated on a deep and abiding black *love*. These responses take the shape of prophetic thought and action: bold, fearless, courageous attempts to tell the truth about and bear witness to black suffering and to keep faith with a vision of black redemption. Like the "ur-texts" of the guttural cry and wrenching moan—enacted in Charlie Parker's bebop sound, Dinah Washington's cool voice, Richard Pryor's comic performances, and James Brown's inimitable funk—the prophetic utterance that focuses on black suffering and sustains a hope-against-hope for black freedom constitutes the heights of black culture. The spiritual depths (the how and what) of Martin Luther King's visionary orations, Nat King Cole's silky soul, August Wilson's probing plays, Martin Puryear's unique sculpture, Harold and Fayard Nicholas's existential acrobatics, Jacob Lawrence's powerful paintings, Marvin Gaye's risky falsettos, Fannie Lou Hamer's fighting songs, and, above all, John Coltrane's *A Love Supreme* exemplify such heights. Two of the greatest moments in black literature also enact such high-quality performances. First, James

Baldwin's great self-descriptive visionary passage in *Go Tell It on the Mountain* (1953):

> Yes, their parts were all cut off, they were dishonored, their very names were nothing more than dust blown disdainfully across the field of time—to fall where, to blossom where, bringing forth what fruit hereafter, where?—their very names were not their own. Behind them was the darkness, nothing but the darkness, and all around them destruction, and before them nothing but the fire—a bastard people, far from God, singing and crying in the wilderness!
>
> Yet, most strangely, and from deeps not before discovered, his faith looked up; before the wickedness that he saw, the wickedness from which he fled, he yet beheld, like a flaming standard in the middle of the air, that power of redemption to which he must, till death, bear witness; which, though it crush him utterly, he could not deny; though none among the living might ever behold it, *he* had beheld it, and must keep the faith.[45]

For Baldwin, the seemingly impossible flight from white supremacy takes the form of a Chekhovian effort to endure lovingly and compassionately, guided by a vision of freedom and empowered by a tradition of black love and faith.[46] To be a bastard people—wrenched from Africa and in, but never fully of, America—is to be a people of highly limited options, if any at all. To bear witness is to make and remake, invent and reinvent oneself as a person and people by keeping faith with the best of such earlier efforts, yet also to acknowledge that the very new selves and peoples to emerge will never fully find a space, place, or face in American society—or Africa. This perennial process of self-making and self-inventing is propelled by a self-loving and self-trusting made possible by overcoming a colonized mind, body and soul.

This is precisely what Toni Morrison describes in the great litany of black love in Baby Suggs's prayer and sermon of laughter, dance, tears, and silence in "a wide-open place cut deep in the woods nobody knew for what at the end of a path known only to deer and whoever cleared the land in the first place." On those hot Saturday afternoons, Baby Suggs "offered up to them her great big heart."

> She told them that the only grace they could have was the grace they could imagine. That if they could not see it, they would not have it.

> "Here," she said, "in this here place, we flesh; flesh that weeps, laughs; flesh that dances on bare feet in grass. Love it. Love it hard. Yonder they do not love your flesh. They despise it. They don't love your eyes; they'd just as soon pick em out. No more do they love the skin on your back. Yonder they flay it. And O my people they do not love your hands. Those they only use, tie, bind, chop off and leave empty. Love your hands! Love them. Raise them up and kiss them. Touch others with them, pat them together, stroke them on your face

'cause they don't love that either. *You* got to love it, *you!* And no, they ain't in love with your mouth. Yonder, out there, they will see it broken and break it again. What you say out of it they will not heed. What you scream from it they do not hear. What you put into it to nourish your body they will snatch away and give you leavins instead. No, they don't love your mouth. *You* got to love it. This is flesh I'm talking about here. Flesh that needs to be loved. Feet that need to rest and to dance; backs that need support; shoulders that need arms, strong arms I'm telling you. And O my people, out yonder, hear me, they do not love your neck unnoosed and straight. So love your neck; put a hand on it, grace it, stroke it and hold it up. And all your inside parts that they'd just as soon slop for hogs, you got to love them. The dark, dark liver—love it, love it, and the beat and beating heart, love that too. More than eyes or feet. More than lungs that have yet to draw free air. More than your life-holding womb and your life-giving private parts, hear me now, love your heart. For this is the prize." Saying no more, she stood up then and danced with her twisted hip the rest of what her heart had to say while the others opened their mouths and gave her the music. Long notes held until the four-part harmony was perfect enough for their deeply loved flesh.[47]

In this powerful passage, Toni Morrison depicts in a concrete and graphic way the enactment and expression of black love, black joy, black community, and black faith that bears witness to black suffering and keeps alive a vision of black hope. Black bonds of affection, black networks of support, black ties of empathy, and black harmonies of spiritual camaraderie provide the grounds for the fragile existential weaponry with which to combat black invisibility and namelessness.

Yet these forceful strategies in black culture still have not successfully come to terms with the problem. The black collective quest for a name that designates black people in the U.S. continues—from colored, Negro, black, Afro-American, Abyssinian, Ethiopian, Nubian, Bilalian, American African, American, African to African American. The black individual quest for names goes on, with unique new ones for children—e.g., Signithia, Tarsell, Jewayne—designed to set them apart from all others for the purpose of accenting their individuality and offsetting their invisibility. And most important, black rage proliferates—sometimes unabated.

Of all the hidden injuries of blackness in American civilization, black rage is the most deadly, the most lethal. Although black culture is in no way reducible to or identical with black rage, it is inseparable from black rage. Du Bois's renowned eulogy for Alexander Crummell, the greatest nineteenth-century black intellectual, is one of the most penetrating analyses of black rage. Du Bois begins his treatment with a virtually generic description of black childhood—a description that would hold for Arthur Ashe or Ice Cube, Kathleen Battle or Queen Latifah.

This is the history of a human heart,—the tale of a black boy who many long years ago began to struggle with life that he might know the world and know himself. Three temptations he met on those dark dunes that lay gray and dismal before the wonder-eyes of the child: the Temptation of Hate, that stood out against the red dawn; the Temptation of Despair, that darkened noonday; and the Temptation of Doubt, that ever steals along with twilight. Above all, you must hear of the vales he crossed,—the Valley of Humiliation and the Valley of the Shadow of Death.[48]

Black self-hatred and hatred of others parallels that of all human beings, who must gain some sense of themselves and the world. But the tremendous weight of white supremacy makes this human struggle for mature black selfhood even more difficult. As black children come to view themselves more and more as the degraded other, the temptation of hate grows, "gliding stealthily into [their] laughter, fading into [their] play, and seizing [their] dreams by day and night with rough, rude turbulence. So [they ask] of sky and sun and flower the never-answered Why? and love, as [they grow], neither the world nor the world's rough ways."[49]

The two major choices in black culture (or any culture) facing those who succumb to the temptation of hate are a self-hatred that leads to self-destruction or a hatred of others—degraded others—that leads to vengeance of some sort. These options often represent two sides of the same coin. The case of Bigger Thomas, portrayed by Richard Wright in his great novel *Native Son* (1940), is exemplary in this regard.

> Bigger's face was metallically black in the strong sunlight. There was in his eyes a pensive, brooding amusement, as of a man who had been long confronted and tantalized by a riddle whose answer seemed always just on the verge of escaping him, but prodding him irresistibly on to seek its solution. The silence irked Bigger; he was anxious to do something to evade looking so squarely at this problem.[50]

The riddle Bigger seeks an answer to is the riddle of his black existence in America—and he evades it in part because the pain, fear, silence, and hatred cuts so deep. Like the "huge black rat" which appears at the beginning of the novel, Bigger reacts to his circumstances instinctually. Yet his instinct to survive is intertwined with his cognitive perception that white supremacy is out to get him. To make himself and invent himself as a black person in America is to strike out against white supremacy—out of pain, fear, silence, and hatred. The result is psychic terror and physical violence—committed against black Bessie and white Mary.

> Bigger rose and went to the window. His hands caught the cold steel bars in a hard grip. He knew as he stood there that he could never tell why he had killed. It was not that he did not really want to tell, but the telling of it would have involved an

explanation of his entire life. The actual killing of Mary and Bessie was not what concerned him most; it was knowing and feeling that he could never make anybody know what had driven him to it. His crimes were known, but what he had felt before he committed them would never be known. He would have gladly admitted his guilt if he had thought that in doing so he could have also given in the same breath a sense of the deep, choking hate that had been his life, a hate that he had not wanted to have, but could not help having. How could he do that? The impulsion to try to tell was as deep as had been the urge to kill.[51]

The temptation to hate is a double-edged sword. Bigger's own self-hatred not only leads him to hate other blacks but also to deny the humanity of whites. Yet he can overcome this self-hatred only when he views himself as a self-determining agent who is willing to take responsibility for his actions and acknowledge his connection with others. Although Wright has often been criticized for casting Bigger as a pitiful victim, subhuman monster, and isolated individualist—as in James Baldwin's "Everybody's Protest Novel" and "Many Thousands Gone" in *Notes of a Native Son* (1955)—Wright presents brief moments in which Bigger sees the need for transcending his victim status and rapacious individualism. When his family visits him in jail, Bigger responds to their tears and anger.

Bigger wanted to comfort them in the presence of the white folks, but did not know how. Desperately, he cast about for something to say. Hate and shame boiled in him against the people behind his back; he tried to think of words that would defy them, words that would let them know that he had a world and life of his own in spite of them.[52]

Wright does not disclose the internal dynamics of this black world of Bigger's own, but Bigger does acknowledge that he is part of this world. For example, his actions had dire consequences for his sister, Vera.

"Bigger," his mother sobbed, trying to talk through her tears. "Bigger, honey, she won't go to school no more. She says the other girls look at her and make her 'shamed. . . ."

He had lived and acted on the assumption that he was alone, and now he saw that he had not been. What he had done made others suffer. No matter how much he would long for them to forget him, they would not be able to. His family was a part of him, not only in blood, but in spirit. He sat on the cot and his mother knelt at his feet. Her face was lifted to his; her eyes were empty, eyes that looked upward when the last hope of earth had failed.[53]

Yet even this family connection fails to undercut the layers of hate Bigger feels for himself and them. It is only when Bigger receives unconditional support and affirmation across racial lines that his self-hatred and hatred of others subsides—for a moment, from white Jan, the boyfriend of the slain Mary.

> He looked at Jan and saw a white face, but an honest face. This white man believed in him, and the moment he felt that belief he felt guilty again; but in a different sense now. Suddenly, this white man had come up to him, flung aside the curtain and walked into the room of his life. Jan had spoken a declaration of friendship that would make other white men hate him: a particle of white rock had detached itself from that looming mountain of white hate and had rolled down the slope, stopping still at his feet. The word had become flesh. For the first time in his life a white man became a human being to him; and the reality of Jan's humanity came in a stab of remorse: he had killed what this man loved and had hurt him. He saw Jan as though someone had performed an operation upon his eyes, or as though someone had snatched a deforming mask from Jan's face.[54]

In both instances, Bigger lurches slightly beyond the temptation of hate when he perceives himself as an agent and subject accountable for the consequences of his actions—such as the victimization of his own black sister and a white person. Yet the depths of his self-hatred—his deep-seated colonized mind—permit only a glimpse of self-transformation when the friendship of a white fellow victim is offered to him.

Similar to Bigger Thomas, Alexander Crummell was inspired by a white significant other—Beriah Green. This sort of sympathetic connection makes the temptation of hate grow "fainter and less sinister. It did not wholly fade away, but diffused itself and lingered thick at the edges."[55] Through both Bigger Thomas and Alexander Crummell we see the tremendous pull of the white world and the tragic need for white recognition and affirmation among so many black people.

The temptation of despair is the second element of black rage in Du Bois's analysis. This temptation looms large when black folk conclude that "the way of the world is closed to me." This conclusion yields two options—nihilism and hedonism. Again, two sides of the same coin. This sense of feeling imprisoned, bound, constrained, and circumscribed is a dominant motif in black cultural expressions.[56] Again, Wright captures this predicament well with Bigger Thomas.

> "Goddammit!"
>
> "What's the matter?"
>
> "They don't let us do *nothing*."
>
> "Who?"
>
> "The *white* folks."
>
> "You talk like you just now finding that out," Gus said.
>
> "Naw. But I just can't get used to it," Bigger said. "I swear to God I can't. I know I oughtn't think about it, but I can't help it. Every time I think about it I feel like somebody's poking a red-hot iron down my throat. Goddammit, look! We live here and they live there. We black and they

white. They got things and we ain't. They do
things and we can't. It's just like living in jail. Half
the time I feel like I'm on the outside of the world
peeping in through a knot-hole in the fence."[57]

The temptation of despair is predicated on a world
with no room for black space, place, or face. It feeds on
a black futurelessness and black hopelessness—a situation in which visions and dreams of possibility have
dried up like raisins in the sun. This nihilism leads to
lives of drift, lives in which any pleasure, especially in-
stant gratification, is the primary means of feeling
alive. Anger and aggression usually surface in such lives.
Bigger says,

I hurt folks 'cause I felt I had to; that's all. They
was crowding me too close; they wouldn't give
me no room. . . . I thought they was hard and I
acted hard. . . . I'll be feeling and thinking that
they didn't see me and I didn't see them.[58]

The major black cultural response to the temptation
of despair has been the black Christian tradition—a
tradition dominated by music in song, prayer, and sermon. The unique role of this tradition is often noted.
Du Bois writes

that the Negro church antedates the Negro home,
leads to an explanation of much that is paradoxical in this communistic institution and in the
morals of its members. But especially it leads us
to regard this institution as peculiarly the expres-

sion of the inner ethical life of a people in a sense seldom true elsewhere.[59]

Even Bigger Thomas—the most cynical and secular of rebels in the black literary tradition—is captivated by the power of black church music, the major caressing artistic flow in the black *Sittlichkeit* (ethical life).

> The singing from the church vibrated through him, suffusing him with a mood of sensitive sorrow. He tried not to listen, but it seeped into his feelings, whispering of another way of life and death. . . . The singing filled his ears; it was complete, self-contained, and it mocked his fear and loneliness, his deep yearning for a sense of wholeness. Its fulness contrasted so sharply with his hunger, its richness with his emptiness, that he recoiled from it while answering it.[60]

The black church tradition—along with the rich musical tradition it spawned—generates a sense of movement, motion, and momentum that keeps despair at bay. As with any collective project or performance that puts a premium on change, transformation, conversion, and future possibility, the temptation of despair is not eliminated but attenuated. In this sense, the black church tradition has made ritual art and communal bonds out of black invisibility and namelessness. Ralph Ellison updates and secularizes this endeavor when he writes,

Perhaps I like Louis Armstrong because he's made poetry out of being invisible. I think it must be because he's unaware that he *is* invisible. And my own grasp of invisibility aids me to understand his music. . . . Invisibility, let me explain, gives one a slightly different sense of time, you're never quite on the beat. Sometimes you're ahead and sometimes behind. Instead of the swift and imperceptible flowing of time, you are aware of its nodes, those points where time stands still or from which it leaps ahead. And you slip into the breaks and look around. That's what you hear vaguely in Louis' music.[61]

The temptation of doubt is the most persistent of the three temptations. White supremacy drums deeply into the hearts, minds, and souls of black people, causing them to expect little of one another and themselves. This black insecurity and self-doubt produces a debilitating black jealousy in the face of black "success"—a black jealousy that often takes the form of what Eldridge Cleaver called "nigger rituals"—namely, a vicious trashing of black "success" or a black "battle royal" for white spectators. Understandably, under conditions of invisibility and namelessness, most of those blacks with "visibility" and a "name" in the white world are often the object of black scorn and contempt. Such sad, self-fulfilling prophecies of black cowardice make the temptation of doubt especially seductive—one which fans and fuels the flames of black rage. Du Bois states,

Of all the three temptations, this one struck the deepest. Hate? He had outgrown so childish a thing. Despair? He had steeled his right arm against it, and fought it with the vigor of determination. But to doubt the worth of his life-work,— to doubt the destiny and capability of the race his soul loved because it was his; to find listless squalor instead of eager endeavor; to hear his own lips whispering, "They do not care; they cannot know; they are dumb driven cattle,—why cast your pearls before swine?"—this, this seemed more than man could bear; and he closed the door, and sank upon the steps of the chancel, and cast his robe upon the floor and writhed.[62]

The two principal options for action after one yields to the temptation of doubt in black culture are: authoritarian subordination of the "ignorant" masses or individual escape from these masses into the white mainstream. These two options are not two sides of the same coin—though they often flow from a common source: an elitist vision that shuns democratic accountability. And although this elitist vision—that of the Exceptional Negro or Talented Tenth who is "better than those other blacks"—is found more readily among the black educated and middle class, some of the black working poor and very poor subscribe to it too. Even Bigger Thomas.

As he rode, looking at the black people on the sidewalks, he felt that one way to end fear and shame was to make all those black people act together, rule them, tell them what to do, and make them do it. . . . But he felt that such would never happen to him and his black people, and he hated them and wanted to wave his hand and blot them out. Yet, he still hoped, vaguely. Of late he had liked to hear tell of men who could rule others, for in actions such as these he felt that there was a way to escape from this tight morass of fear and shame that sapped at the base of his life. He liked to hear of how Japan was conquering China; of how Hitler was running Jews to the ground; of how Mussolini was invading Spain. He was not concerned with whether these acts were right or wrong; they simply appealed to him as possible avenues of escape. He felt that some day there would be a black man who would whip the black people into a tight band and together they would act and end fear and shame. He never thought of this in precise mental images; he felt it; he would feel it for a while and then forget. But hope was always waiting somewhere deep down in him.[63]

This hope for black unity and action was based on a profound doubt concerning the ability of black people to think for themselves and act on principles they had examined, scrutinized, and deliberately chosen. Ironically, this same elitist logic is at work among those who uncritically enter the white mainstream and accuse black people of lacking discipline and determination. Alexander Crummell overcame the difficult challenge of self-doubt and the doubt of other black folk by moving to Africa and later returning to America to fight for and "among his own, the low, the grasping, and the wicked, with that unbending righteousness which is the sword of the just."[64]

In the end, for Du Bois, Alexander Crummell triumphed over hate, despair, and doubt owing to "that full power within, that mighty inspiration"[65] within the Veil. He was able to direct his black rage through moral channels sustained primarily by black bonds of affection, black networks of support, and black ties of empathy. Yet few today know his name and work, principally due to the thick Veil of color then and now.

> His name today, in this broad land, means little, and comes to fifty million ears laden with no incense of memory or emulation. And herein lies the tragedy of the age: not that men are poor,—all men know something of poverty; not that men are wicked,—who is good? not that men are ignorant,—what is Truth? Nay, but that men know so little of men.[66]

For Du Bois, "the problem of the twentieth century is the problem of the color-line"[67] largely because of the relative lack of communication across the Veil of color. For Du Bois, the vicious legacy of white supremacy contributes to the arrested development of democracy. And since communication is the lifeblood of a democracy—the very measure of the vitality of its public life—we either come to terms with race and hang together, or ignore it and hang separately. This is why every examination of black strivings is an important part of understanding the prevailing crisis in American society.

A TWILIGHT CIVILIZATION

IN OUR TIME—at the end of the twentieth century—the crisis of race in America is still raging. The problem of black invisibility and namelessness, however, remains marginal to the dominant accounts of our past and present and is relatively absent from our pictures of the future. In this age of globalization, with its impressive scientific and technological innovations in information, communication, and applied biology, a focus on the lingering effects of racism seems outdated and antiquated. The global cultural bazaar of entertainment and enjoyment, the global shopping mall of advertising and marketing, the global workplace of blue-collar and white-collar employment, and the global financial network of computerized transactions and megacorporate mergers appear to render any talk about race irrelevant.[68]

Yet with the collapse of the Soviet Empire, the end of the Cold War, and the rise of Japan, corrupt and top-heavy nation-states are being eclipsed by imperial corporations as public life deteriorates due to class polarization, racial balkanization, and especially a predatory market culture.[69] With the vast erosion of civic networks that nurture and care for citizens—such as families, neighborhoods, and schools—and with what might be called the gangsterization of everyday life, characterized by the escalating fear of violent attack, vicious assault, or cruel insult, we are witnessing a pervasive cultural decay in American civilization. Even public discourse has degenerated into petty name-calling and finger-pointing—with little room for mutual respect and empathetic exchange. Increasing suicides and homicides, alcoholism and drug addiction, distrust and disloyalty, coldheartedness and mean-spiritedness, isolation and loneliness, cheap sexual thrills and cowardly patriarchal violence are still other symptoms of this decay. Yet race—in the coded language of welfare reform, immigration policy, criminal punishment, affirmative action, and suburban privatization—remains a central signifier in the political debate.

As in late nineteenth-century Russia and early twentieth-century Central Europe, the ruling political right hides and conceals the privilege and wealth of the few (the 1 percent who own 48 percent of the net financial wealth, the top 10 percent who own 86 percent, the top 20 percent who have 94 percent!) and pits the downwardly mobile middlers against the downtrodden poor.[70] This age-old strategy of scapegoating the most vulnerable, frightening the most insecure, and supporting the most comfortable constitutes a kind of iron law signaling the decline of modern civilizations, as in Tolstoy's Russia and Kafka's Central Europe: chaotic and inchoate rebellion from below, withdrawal and retreat from public life from above, and a desperate search for authoritarian law and order, at any cost, from the middle. In America, this suggests not so much a European style of fascism but rather a homespun brand of authoritarian democracy—the systemic stigmatizing, regulating, and policing of the degraded "others"—women, gays, lesbians, Latinos, Jews, Asians, Indians, and especially black people. As Sinclair Lewis warned over a half-century ago, fascism, American-style, can happen here.

Welfare reform means, on the ground, poor people (disproportionately black) with no means of support. Criminal punishment means hundreds of thousands of black men in crowded prisons—many in there forever. And suburban privatization means black urban poor citizens locked into decrepit public schools, dilapidated housing, inadequate health care, and unavailable child care. Furthermore, the lowest priorities on the global corporate agenda of the political right—the low quantity of jobs with a living wage and the low quality of life for children—have the gravest consequences for the survival of any civilization. Instead, we have generational layers of unemployed and underemployed people (often uncounted in our national statistics) and increasing numbers of hedonistic and nihilistic young people (of all classes, races, genders, and regions) with little interest in public life and with little sense of moral purpose.

This is the classic portrait of a twilight civilization whose dangerous rumblings—now intermittent in much of America but rampant in most of black urban America—will more than likely explode in the twenty-first century if we stay on the present conservative course. In such a bleak scenario—given the dominant tendencies of our day—Du Bois's heralded Talented Tenth will by and large procure a stronger foothold in the well-paid professional managerial sectors of the global economy and more and more will become intoxicated with the felicities of a parvenu bourgeois existence. The heroic few will attempt to tell unpleasant truths about our plight and bear prophetic witness to our predicament as well as try to organize and mobilize (and be organized and mobilized by) the economically devastated, culturally degraded, and politically marginalized black working poor and very poor. Since a multiracial alliance of progressive middlers, liberal slices of the corporate elite, and subversive energy from below is the only vehicle by which some form of radical democratic accountability can redistribute resources and wealth and restructure the economy and government so that all benefit, the significant secondary efforts of the black Talented Tenth alone in the twenty-first century will be woefully inadequate and thoroughly frustrating. Yet even progressive social change—though desirable and necessary—may not turn back the deeper and deadly processes of cultural decay in late twentieth-century America.

As this Talented Tenth comes to be viewed more and more with disdain and disgust by the black working poor and very poor, not only class envy but class hatred in black America will escalate—in the midst of a more isolated and insulated black America. This will deepen the identity crisis of the black Talented Tenth—a crisis of survivor's guilt and cultural rootlessness. As the glass ceilings (limited promotions) and golden cuffs (big position and good pay with little or no power) remain in place for most, though not all, blacks in corporate America, we will see anguish and hedonism intensify among much of the Talented Tenth. The con-

servative wing of black elites will climb on the band-
wagon of the political right—some for sincere reasons,
most for opportunistic ones—as the black working
poor and very poor try to cope with the realities of
death, disease, and destruction. The progressive wing
of the black elite will split into a vociferous (primarily
male-led) black nationalist camp that opts for self-help
at the lower and middle levels of the entrepreneurial
sectors of the global economy and a visionary (disproportionately woman-led) radical democratic camp that
works assiduously to keep alive a hope—maybe the
last hope—for a twilight civilization that once saw itself as the "last best hope of earth."

After ninety-five years of the most courageous and
unflagging devotion to black freedom witnessed in the
twentieth century, W. E. B. Du Bois not only left America for Africa but concluded,

> I just cannot take any more of this country's treat-
> ment. We leave for Ghana October 5th and I set
> no date for return. . . . Chin up, and fight on, but
> realize that American Negroes can't win.[71]

In the end, Du Bois's Enlightenment worldview, Victorian strategies, and American optimism failed him.
He left America in militant despair—the very despair
he had avoided earlier—and mistakenly hoped for the
rise of a strong postcolonial and united Africa. Echoing Tolstoy's claim that "it's intolerable to live in Russia. . . . I've decided to emigrate to England forever"[72]
(though he never followed through) and Kafka's dream
to leave Prague and live in Palestine (though he died

before he could do so),[73] Du Bois concluded that black strivings in a twilight civilization were unbearable for him yet still imperative for others—even if he could not envision black freedom in America as realizable.

For those of us who stand on his broad shoulders, let us begin where he ended—with his militant despair; let us look candidly at the tragicomic and absurd character of black life in America in the spirit of John Coltrane and Toni Morrison; let us continue to strive with genuine compassion, personal integrity, and human decency to fight for radical democracy in the face of the frightening abyss—or terrifying inferno—of the twenty-first century, clinging to "a hope not hopeless but unhopeful."

APPENDIX

W. E. B. Du Bois
and "The Talented Tenth"

WHEN W. E. B. Du Bois published his polemical book of essays, *The Souls of Black Folk,* in 1903, he became the second great African-American public intellectual. Frederick Douglass, the ex-slave abolitionist, sublime orator, and critically acclaimed autobiographer—and one of only two other black intellectuals whom Du Bois would acknowledge as antecedents—was the first. In his curiously compelling little book, Du Bois was able to achieve something unprecedented in African-American letters: he was able, in fourteen lyrical essays, framed by a mystical "Forethought" and "Afterthought," to give a narrative voice and shape to the "nationhood"—the status as a "nation-within-a-nation"—of eight million descendants of both the African past and human bondage, flung together from hundreds of cultures and geographical locations, from Senegambia and the Gold Coast to Angola and the Congo, and forged into a new people, *sui generis,* in the harsh cauldron of chattel, race-based slavery in the New World.

Practically overnight, *Souls* was hailed as a monumental achievement, a classic work by any standard: through myth and metaphor, and in a densely lyrical yet polemical prose, the young Du Bois charted the contours of the civilization—the arts and sciences, the metaphysical and religious systems, the myths and music, the social and political institutions, the history both before and after Emancipation—that defined a truly African-American culture at the outset of the new century. Du Bois did nothing less than narrate a black dual nationhood: a nationality at once American yet paradoxically and resonantly African-American.

A. C. McClurg and Company of Chicago published *The Souls of Black Folk* on April 18, 1903, just two months after the author's thirty-fifth birthday. Between 1903 and 1905, no fewer than six printings of the book were necessary to satisfy demand. Despite his young age, the author, William Edward Burghardt Du Bois (1868–1963), had become by the turn of the century "one of the two or three best-known Afro-Americans in the nation," as the historian Herbert Aptheker accurately observes. Indeed, Du Bois's emergence as a dominant political figure in the Afro-American community is without parallel in the history of black leadership, because his vehicle to prominence was not the deed, or the spoken word; it was the written word. Even his contemporaries realized how curious his route to power had been; as the Afro-American educator William H. Ferris, a Yale graduate, put the matter in *The African Abroad* in 1913:

> Du Bois is one of the few men in history who was hurled on the throne of leadership by the dynamic force of the written word. He is one of the few writers who leaped to the front as a leader and became the head of a popular movement through impressing his personality upon men by means of a book.

What's more, Ferris concludes, Du Bois's ascendancy was inadvertent: "He had no aspiration of becoming a race leader when he wrote his *Souls of Black Folk*. But that book has launched him upon a brilliant career."

The publication of *Souls* marked a high point in Du Bois's phenomenal career, which had begun with his graduation from Fisk University in 1888. At his graduation from Harvard in 1890, where he took a B.A., cum laude, in philosophy (he had taken his first A.B. at Fisk), he delivered one of the five commencement orations. The address, on Jefferson Davis, received extraordinarily broad mention in the national press. In the fall of that year, he entered the Harvard graduate school. While an undergraduate at Harvard, his principal mentors had been William James and George Santayana (philosophy), Frank Taussig (economics), and Albert Bushnell Hart (history). Du Bois's first love was philosophy. But because employment opportunities were limited for black philosophers, he decided on graduate study in history. Study in Europe had long been Du Bois's dream; in October 1892, having earned an M.A. in history at Harvard the year before, he enrolled at Friedrich Wilhelm University in Berlin, studying sociology, economics, history, and political theory.

Berlin was all that he had hoped for academically; Du Bois enjoyed the challenging rigor of his work there, including lectures by the great sociologist Max Weber, who would remain a close friend. (In 1904, Weber would participate in Du Bois's annual conference at Atlanta University on the status of the Negro.) Du Bois wrote a thesis on agricultural economics in the South and ardently desired to take a Ph.D. Unable to do so (because of a residency requirement that he was unable to satisfy due to lack of funds), Du Bois returned to the United States and began to teach the classics at Wilberforce University, in Xenia, Ohio. A year later, in 1895, the year Frederick Douglass died, he became the first person of African descent to take a Ph.D. from Harvard.

Du Bois's next eight years were exceptionally productive. In 1896, he published his doctoral dissertation, *The Suppression of the African Slave Trade to the United States of America, 1638–1870*, as volume 1 of the Harvard Historical Monograph Series. That autumn, he moved to the University of Pennsylvania to undertake a sociological study of the Negro population of Philadelphia. One year later, he joined with Alexander Crummell and other black scholars in founding the American Negro Academy, the very first black institute of arts and letters in the world.

In the fall of 1897, Du Bois commenced a professorship of economics and history at Atlanta University, where he assumed the directorship of the "Atlanta Conferences," convened annually to generate precise scientific research about the actual living conditions of Negroes in America, about whom surprisingly little sound scientific data existed. Du Bois edited the products of these conferences and published them in a monograph series, between 1889 and 1914, in sixteen volumes. His intention was to collect, collate, and analyze socioeconomic data about every conceivable facet of black life in America. This project was a bold, imaginative venture, one motivated by Du Bois's belief that ignorance, rather than a primal xenophobia or economic relationships, was the primary cause of racism. Du Bois would much later abandon that view, deciding that material relationships—especially economic scarcity—masked themselves in the guise of race relationships.

In 1899, the results of his sociological research at the University of Pennsylvania were published as *The Philadelphia Negro*. Between 1897 and 1903, Du Bois, starting with an essay printed in the *Atlantic Monthly*, became one of the most widely published authors in the United States. His essays appeared in such prominent publications as *The Independent*, *The Nation*, *The Southern Workman*, *Harper's Weekly*, *World's Work*, *The Outlook*, *The Missionary Review*, *The Literary Digest*, the *Annals of the American Academy of Political and Social Science*, and

The Dial, among other magazines and journals. He was a polymath.

By 1903, then, Du Bois not only could count himself among the most deeply read, most widely traveled, and most broadly and impeccably educated human beings in the world, he had also become the most widely published black essayist in the history of African Americans since the abolitionist campaign led by Frederick Douglass. Du Bois was, more than any other figure—including his nemesis, Booker T. Washington (the founder of the Tuskegee Institute and the dominant political force in Negro politics between 1895 and 1915)—the public written "voice" of the Negro American intellectual.

Despite the powerful achievement of *Souls,* however, in it Du Bois had failed to account adequately for class differences within the black community, the differences that resulted from broadly diverse access to education among blacks themselves, and the implications of these differentials of education, income, customs, habits, and philosophies. For if, in an age of oppression unparalleled since the collapse of slavery in 1865, an age that the historian Rayford Logan would call "the nadir" in African-American history; if, in this age of Black Codes and the birth of Jim Crow segregation, sanctioned as recently as 1896 by the Supreme Court in the infamous *Plessy v. Ferguson* decision; if blacks were defined before the law as members of one undifferentiated class, *within* the African-American nation, class structures were at least a century or more old. To address the relations among these classes—the social and ethical responsibilities that black "haves" bore to black "have-nots"—in 1903 Du Bois also published his essay "The Talented Tenth," which can be read as a coda to *The Souls of Black Folk.*

Du Bois had been preparing this large statement since the death of Frederick Douglass in 1895. Eighteen ninety-five would prove to be a momentous year in Du Bois's life, for in that year he not only would bury his first hero, he would insert another, Alexander Crummell, in his place. The work of both would be central in shaping his thinking about the ethical role of black intellectuals generally, and would especially inform his thoughts about the Talented Tenth.

Du Bois was deeply moved when, on February 20, 1895, he received news of Douglass's death. In his grief, he was moved on that night to write and rewrite a series of elegies to Douglass, feeling the weight of the mantle that, secretly, he felt to be his. Over and over, Du Bois struggled with the poems' tone, with the image of death and the legacy of tradition. If Douglass's mantle would be a burden, it was a burden he longed to bear. Douglass haunted Du Bois, dogging his steps as the model to be emulated, and as a counterforce to Booker T. Washington's theories of laissez-faire economics and laissez-faire political accommodation.

Du Bois had every reason to be anxious about this. Just a few months after Douglass's death, Booker T. Washington would deliver his infamous "Atlanta Exposition" speech, catapulting himself into a position as the conservative leader of the black community. Even Du Bois's beloved Harvard would award Washington an honorary A.M. degree in 1896. For the turn-of-the-century black neo-abolitionists, Douglass's legacy was in grave danger of being dismantled by one of their own.

Du Bois eulogized Douglass at a memorial service at Wilberforce University, and shortly following the publication of *The Souls of Black Folk,* he agreed to write a biography of Douglass in a series being published by the

George W. Jacobs publishing company of Philadelphia. Jacobs withdrew this offer early in 1904, when Booker T. Washington accepted the company's earlier invitation, which had remained unanswered until Du Bois accepted, thus robbing Du Bois of the opportunity to immortalize Douglass as he had Alexander Crummell just a few months before.

Alexander Crummell was the first African American to take a bachelor's degree from the University of Cambridge, an Episcopal priest who served twenty years in Liberia, and, after 1873, the rector of St. Luke's Episcopal Church in Washington, D.C., which President Chester A. Arthur occasionally attended. Most important, however, for Du Bois, Crummell in 1897 founded, and served as the first president of, the American Negro Academy.

Du Bois never met Frederick Douglass; his first meeting with Crummell, on the other hand, was one of the truly germinal moments in his intellectual life. He would immortalize that day, and the awe that Crummell had inspired, in the essay "Of Alexander Crummell," which he published in *The Souls of Black Folk*.

Du Bois would pay ultimate tribute both to Douglass and to Crummell in what is perhaps the most fitting way of all: he grounded his essay "The Talented Tenth" in two essays written by his mentors—Douglass's 1854 address "The Claims of the Negro Ethnologically Considered" and one of Crummell's central works, "Civilization: The Primal Need of the Race," his inaugural address as president of the American Negro Academy, delivered in 1897.

In Douglass's address, a remarkably prescient speech made to the scholars at Western Reserve College, he had asserted the fundamental equality of all members of the human species; the underlying unity of black cultures in Africa and the New World; the social construction of difference; the role of environment, as opposed to genetics, in the shaping of human intelligence; and the antiquity of black cultures, traceable to the ancient Egyptians:

> It is somewhat remarkable, that, at a time when knowledge is so generally diffused, when the geography of the world is so well understood—when time and space, in the intercourse of nations, are almost annihilated—when oceans have become bridges—the earth a magnificent hall—the hollow sky a dome—under which a common humanity can meet in friendly conclave—when nationalities are being swallowed up—and the ends of the earth brought together—I say it is remarkable—nay, it is strange that there should arise a phalanx of learned men—speaking in the name of *science*—to forbid the magnificent reunion of mankind in one brotherhood. A mortifying proof is here given, that the moral growth of a nation, or an age, does not always keep pace with the increase of knowledge, and suggests the necessity of means to increase human love with human learning.

From Alexander Crummell, Du Bois took the following sentiment, which could have served as the epigraph of his 1903 essay: "The primal need of the Negro is absorption in civilization, in all its several lines, as a preparation for civil functions, and the use of political power. Just now he is the puppet and the tool of white demagogues and black sycophants." As David Levering Lewis shows so well in his stellar *W. E. B. Du Bois: Biography of a Race,* Crummell knew that nationalism was the proverbial figure in the carpet for black intellectuals. As Lewis writes, Crummell identified "two great heresies" within black intellectual thought: "that the colored people of this country should forget as soon as possible that they ARE colored people," and "that colored men should give up all distinctive efforts as colored men, in schools, churches, associations, and friendly societies." Moreover, "If I forget that I am a black man, and you ignore the fact of race, and we both, ostrich-like, stick our heads in the sand . . . what are you and I to do for our social nature?" Negroes in America, he concluded, "are a nation set apart in this country."

In "The Conservation of Races," a speech to the American Negro Academy that followed Crummell's in 1897, Du Bois articulated two ideas that would prove to be pivotal in his early career, and which would be central to the argument put forth in "The Talented Tenth." The first was his critique of Jeffersonian individualism, the notion that in America, for the first time, rights and duties were individual-based, not group-based. Not so, Du Bois declared. The Negro, he argued, had been brought to these shores as forced labor, by definition, as a member of a group; he or she experienced oppression, by definition, as a member of this group; custom, practice, and even, in the case of the Negro, the law had "silently but definitely separated men into groups," and among these groups, precisely because of their internal histories as well as their external treatment, there existed cultural and social differences, "subtle, delicate and elusive, though they may be."

Du Bois then made his most important argument, in which he attempted to define the relation between what T. S. Eliot would two decades later call "tradition and the individual talent": "The history of the world is the history, not of individuals, but of groups, not of nations, but of races, and he who ignores or seeks to override the race idea in human history ignores and overrides the central thought of all history." Tradition, Du Bois argues, is a cultural construct, one inextricably tied to the concept of nationhood.

Du Bois proceeded to paint a vast canvas of a truly multicultural world, with each nation, or "race," assigned its own, equal subjectivity in Nature's grand work of art, a genuinely humane world civilization. The American Negro bore a relation to Negroes in Africa, he wrote, similar to that which the intellectual and professional elite within "the race"—"the advanced guard," as he would put it time and time again—bore to those less fortunate victims of slavery and segregation who comprised the bulk of African Americans at the turn of the century.

Just as African Americans were the vanguard of the world's Negro peoples, so too were the members of the intellectual class simultaneously the most representative members of, and the natural leaders of, the American Negro people. And it is as Negroes, as an African people in the New World, first and foremost, that we exist, Du Bois argued.

[W]hat after all, am I? Am I an American or am I a Negro? Can I be both? Or is it my duty to cease to be a Negro as soon as possible and be an American? If I strive as a Negro, am I not perpetuating the very cleft that threatens and separates black and white America? Is not my only possible practical aim the subduction of all that is Negro in me to the American? Does my black blood place upon me any more obligation to assert my nationality than German, or Irish or Italian blood would? . . .

Here it seems to me, is the reading of the riddle that puzzles so many of us. We are Americans, not only by birth and by citizenship, but by our political ideals, our language, our religion. Farther than that, our Americanism does not go. At that point, we are Negroes, members of a vast historic race that from the very dawn of creation has slept, but half awakening in the dark forests of its African fatherland. We are the first fruits of this new nation, the harbinger of that black tomorrow which is yet destined to soften the whiteness of the Teutonic today.

The relation between the black individual and the group, he argued, is that between the part and the whole. Oppression by groups—three centuries of such oppression—has led to cultural, social, and political organization by groups, especially since the rights of the Negro individual (as the Supreme Court had reminded the larger society just the year before in the 1896 *Plessy v. Ferguson* decision, which affirmed "separate but equal" as a reasonable doctrine applying to social relations between blacks and whites) were almost entirely subsumed under rights accorded, or denied, the Negro as a group.

These central ideas became the scaffolding of the structure outlined in Du Bois's blueprint for the duties and obligations of Negro leadership which he developed in "The Talented Tenth." The phrase itself Du Bois appropriated from Henry Morehouse (as historian Evelyn Brooks-Higginbotham has shown), who coined the term in 1896, one year after Booker T. Washington delivered his famous speech enunciating the tenets of political and social accommodation at the Atlanta Exposition, the year of *Plessy v. Ferguson*. Morehouse, the executive secretary of the American Baptist Home Mission Society between 1879 and 1893 and again between 1902 and 1917, in an article printed in *The Independent* wrote:

I repeat that not to make proper provision for the high education of the talented tenth man of the colored colleges is a prodigious mistake. It is to dwarf the tree that has in it the promise of a grand oak. Industrial education is good for the nine; the common English branches are good for the nine; that tenth man ought to have the best opportunities for making the most of himself for humanity and God.

It was this concept of "the tenth man" that Du Bois would modify so dramatically in his attempt to define for a small, but rising, middle class what precisely its obligations and responsibilities to the larger black community were.

"The Talented Tenth" was Du Bois's response to Jefferson's notion of a "natural aristocracy," those endowed, by nature, with the innate talent and opportunities to lead, to excel. To speak of a "tenth" of the Negro people as conforming to any reasonable definition of a middle class was optimistic, to say the least. By 1917, for example, only 2,132 black Americans were attending college; in 1900, just over 2,000 held college degrees, while 21,000 blacks were schoolteachers. By 1930, according to historian Carter G. Woodson, there were 1,748 black physicians, 1,230 lawyers, and 2,131 academic administrators, "with some hundreds of bankers, businessmen, engineers, architects, and scientists." As David Levering Lewis puts it, Du Bois seems to be referring to the "million men of Negro blood, well-educated, owners of homes . . . who, judged by any standard, have reached the full measure of the best type of modern European culture." "A far more accurate characterization," Lewis concludes, "would have been the Talented Hundredth." Curiously enough, in 1948, Du Bois himself, in a rereading of his own 1903 essay, modified the phrase to just that: "the Guiding Hundredth."

When Du Bois wrote "The Talented Tenth," blacks comprised 11.6 percent of the population. The 1900 U.S. Census had counted 8,833,944 Negroes. Of these, approximately 90 percent lived in the South, while only 25 percent lived in urban areas. Life expectancy for black men and women was thirty-four years, compared to forty-eight years for white men and women. Illiteracy among blacks was 44.5 percent.

The nation had legally abandoned the fundamental principles of Reconstruction in the *Plessy* decision of 1896, having abandoned them politically in the Hayes-Tilden Compromise exactly two decades before. From 1896 to 1903, at least 730 blacks were reported lynched. In 1898, Georgia inaugurated something it called "the white primary," in which only whites could vote in Democratic primary contests. Louisiana adopted a "grandfather clause" in its state constitution; as a result, the number of blacks registered to vote in that state dropped from 130,344 in 1896 to 5,320 in 1900. The Supreme Court, true to the mold cast in *Plessy* two years before, upheld the poll tax (in *Williams v. Mississippi*) as constitutional. The first anti-lynching bill, introduced in 1900 in Congress by George H. White, failed to get out of committee. One year later, White's second term ended, ending black representation in Congress until 1928. To say that the status of Negroes was at its "nadir," as the historian Rayford Logan put it, when Du Bois wrote his essay is to understate their perilous condition.

"The Talented Tenth" was published in a book of essays entitled *The Negro Problem: A Series of Articles by Representative American Negroes of Today,* thought to have been edited, or at least endorsed, by Du Bois's nemesis, Booker T. Washington himself. In addition to essays by Washington and Du Bois, the book includes pieces by Charles W. Chesnutt, Wilford H. Smith, H. T. Kealing, Paul Laurence Dunbar, and T. Thomas Fortune. Washington's presence in that volume and probable sponsorship makes Du Bois's opening paragraph all the more daring, amounting as it did to a direct challenge both to Washington's political ideology and to his stance on the Negro's education.

Du Bois's essay is structured in three parts: part one is a brisk trot through the great men and women theory of black history; part two is Du Bois's effort to show how American society can expand this "class of men," as he puts it elsewhere; and part three contains Du Bois's theory of the relation of these leaders "to the Negro problem."

Du Bois, in the first section of his essay, points to the remarkable achievements against the greatest odds of a host of leading figures in African-American arts and letters, science, politics, business, and religion—figures of "moral regeneration," as Du Bois puts it. He does so in part to show how American society can increase the size of this group of achievers (which he will elaborate upon in part two of the essay). But his essay—as well as the book in which it was printed—is also aimed in part at those white industrialists who had been such staunch supporters of Washington, who had built his castle and his moat. It was because of their vast ignorance about black history that he undertook this excursion through great black lives.

Negro leadership is "exceptional," Du Bois continues, not because of hereditary or natural inferiority but because of the hideous effects of custom and environment, especially the pernicious history of slavery and practice of Jim Crow racism that was reemerging at the turn of the century, even as Du Bois writes his essay. To those who point to statistics concerning black poverty—of death, disease, and "crime"—and argue that this is "the happy rule," Du Bois counters:

Of course they are the rule, because a silly nation made them the rule: Because for three long centuries this people lynched Negroes who dared to be brave, raped black women who dared to be virtuous, crushed dark-hued youth who dared to be ambitious, and encouraged and made to flourish servility and lewdness and apathy.

Rid the society of racism, Du Bois argues, and the socio-economic roots of the supposed "moral degeneracy" of Negroes will be exposed. Blacks not limited by these conditions, he concludes, will thrive, in proportions similar to the success ratios of every other ethnic group in America.

Finally, in the essay's third section, Du Bois outlines the ethical functions of black leadership, "the function of the college-bred Negro": "He is, as he ought to be, the group leader, the man who sets the ideals of the community where he lives, directs its thoughts and heads its social movements."

So far, so good. But here Du Bois overstates the case, attempting to persuade even the most skeptical or hostile racist, by appearing to accept the racist premise that the Negro people need social leadership more than most groups, because they have no traditions, customs, or strong family ties of their own. To make his case, Du Bois granted his readers certain assumptions about Negro culture, which would later be developed by sociologists in the tradition of Robert Parks, who tended to stress the "pathological" side of segregated black life. Separate, by definition, was unequal because social and cultural separation and isolation, born of slavery and Jim Crow segregation, had a dehumanizing effect upon their victims. And just as he had done in "Of the Conservation of Races" six years before, Du Bois ended "The Talented Tenth" with an appeal to Americans to support his argument not for the sake of the Negro, but because it made good social and economic sense for themselves.

Du Bois felt, rightly, that Negro Americans were under siege, aided and abetted, wittingly or unwittingly, by Booker T. Washington and his followers, who, Du Bois felt, were all too eager to further their own agendas by taking a set of ideological positions which reinforced the larger society's apparent tendency to disenfranchise the Negro and reverse the gains of Reconstruction. To appeal to even the most conservative supporters of Washington, then, Du Bois accepted the premise that much of black culture was depraved (if depraved for environmental reasons), all the better to draw a contrast with those in the race who were not depraved, hence defeating any attempt to ascribe these social or cultural "characteristics" to nature. He was also quite comfortable with the notion of elites within all groups: there were black natural aristocrats as well as white ones.

While no one has ever accused Du Bois of being egalitarian, he did seek to qualify these statements in his own rejoinder to his 1903 essay, in a speech he delivered at the Nineteenth Grand Boulé Conclave in 1948. Du Bois is at pains to do two things straightaway: first, to put to rest any idea that he had intended to be elitist in 1903, and second, to stress the notion of "service" implicit in the "call" of leadership in the black community. "It has been said that I had in mind the building of an aristocracy with neglect of the masses," he confesses. "I assumed that with knowledge, sacrifice would automatically follow. In my youth and idealism," he admits, "I did not realize that selfishness is even more natural than sacrifice."

No, the members of the Talented Tenth must "work not simply as individuals," individuals motivated primarily by "personal freedom and unhampered enjoyment and use of the world, without any real care . . . as to what became of the mass of American Negroes, or of the mass of any people." Du Bois wishes to emphasize group responsibility, for a collective economic, as well as cultural, entity, which would plan "for such economic revolution in industry and just distribution of wealth, as would make the rise of our group possible."

To demonstrate what is at the basis of this relation of part to whole, of individual to the group, Du Bois defines what he means by "race," a concept, as Kwame Anthony Appiah has so deftly demonstrated, with which he grappled uneasily throughout his writing career. Du Bois argues that black people are not merely related physically but culturally. He explains, "I came then to advocate, not pride of biological race, but pride in a cultural group, integrated and expanded by developed ideals."

However, Du Bois recognizes the paradox that a century's agitation for full civil rights, coupled with the systematic racist disparagement of black culture, had led to a black cultural elite often eager to become Americans that they sometimes appeared to deny the existence of a Negro culture: "The leadership, then, of my Talented Tenth over the mass of young colored men and women, college-trained and entering their careers, faced rejection and disappearance of the Negro, both as a race and as a culture."

Such a nation-within-a-nation, he concludes, echoing Alexander Crummell, a "nation" larger than Canada, Saudi Arabia, Hungary, the Netherlands, South Africa, Ethiopia, Australia, or Switzerland, cannot simply disappear or erase itself as one of the world's great cultures.

Who is to lead in the preservation of this great culture and, in the process—a process as necessary in 1948 as it was in 1903—demand an end to the socioeconomic conditions afflicting the mass of the black community? Here Du Bois substitutes the phrase "group-leadership" for "the

Talented Tenth," by which he means a well-educated, "self-sacrificing," cosmopolitan elite in "alliance with culture groups in Europe, America, Asia, and Africa, and looking toward a new world culture." This group of leaders, if not precisely socialist, then social democrats or "liberals," he concludes, "can free our own mass by organization and group influence exercised through a self-sacrificing leadership. This is primarily a question of character," he admits, "which I failed to emphasize in my first proposal of a Talented Tenth."

This new Talented Tenth, then, while remaining an elite, a vanguard, is acutely aware of its social and ethical obligations to the larger group, its members keenly aware that their privileged positions stem not from their own inherent nobility of mind and spirit but from "opportunity." There, but for the grace of God, Du Bois maintains, pointing to the plight of the black lower classes, goes even the Talented Tenth.

Henry Louis Gates, Jr.

"THE TALENTED TENTH"
W. E. B. Du Bois

(published in The Negro Problem, *1903)*

THE NEGRO RACE, like all races, is going to be saved by its exceptional men. The problem of education, then, among Negroes must first of all deal with the Talented Tenth; it is the problem of developing the Best of this race that they may guide the Mass away from the contamination and death of the Worst, in their own and other races. Now the training of men is a difficult and intricate task. Its technique is a matter for educational experts, but its object is for the vision of seers. If we make money the object of man-training, we shall develop money-makers but not necessarily men; if we make technical skill the object of education, we may possess artisans but not, in nature, men. Men we shall have only as we make manhood the object of the work of the schools—intelligence, broad sympathy, knowledge of the world that was and is, and of the relation of men to it—this is the curriculum of that Higher Education which must underlie true life. On this foundation we may build bread winning, skill of hand and quickness of brain, with never a fear lest the child and man mistake the means of living for the object of life.

If this be true—and who can deny it—three tasks lay before me; first to show from the past that the Talented Tenth as they have risen among American Negroes have been worthy of leadership; secondly, to show how these men may be educated and developed; and thirdly, to show their relation to the Negro problem.

You misjudge us because you do not know us. From the very first it has been the educated and intelligent of the Negro people that have led and elevated the mass, and the sole obstacles that nullified and retarded their efforts were slavery and race prejudice; for what is slavery but the legalized survival of the unfit and the nullification of the work of natural internal leadership? Negro leadership, therefore, sought from the first to rid the race of this awful incubus that it might make way for natural selection and the survival of the fittest. In colonial days came Phillis Wheatley and Paul Cuffe striving against the bars of prejudice; and Benjamin Banneker, the almanac maker, voiced their longings when he said to Thomas Jefferson, "I freely and cheerfully acknowledge that I am of the African Race, and in colour which is natural to them, of the deepest dye; and it is under a sense of the most profound gratitude to the Supreme Ruler of the Universe, that I now confess to you that I am not under that state of tyrannical thraldom and inhuman captivity to which too many of my brethren are doomed, but that I have abundantly tasted of the fruition of those blessings which proceed from that free and unequalled liberty with which you are favored, and which I hope you will willingly allow, you have mercifully received from the immediate hand of that Being from whom proceedeth every good and perfect gift.

"Suffer me to recall to your mind that time, in which the arms of the British crown were exerted with every powerful effort, in order to reduce you to a state of servitude; look back, I entreat you, on the variety of dangers to which you were exposed; reflect on that period in which every human aid appeared unavailable, and in which even hope and fortitude wore the aspect of inability to the conflict, and you cannot but be led to a serious and grateful sense of your miraculous and providential preservation, you cannot but acknowledge, that the present freedom and tranquility which you enjoy, you have mercifully received, and that a peculiar blessing of heaven.

"This, sir, was a time when you clearly saw into the injustice of a state of Slavery, and in which you had just apprehensions of the horrors of its condition. It was then that your abhorrence thereof was so excited, that you publicly held forth this true and invaluable doctrine, which is worthy to be recorded and remembered in all succeeding ages: 'We hold these truths to be self evident, that all men are created equal; that they are endowed with certain inalienable rights, and that among these are life, liberty and the pursuit of happiness.' "

Then came Dr. James Derham, who could tell even the learned Dr. Rush something of medicine, and Lemuel Haynes, to whom Middlebury gave an honorary A.M. in 1804. These and others we may call the Revolutionary group of distinguished Negroes—they were persons of marked ability, leaders of a Talented Tenth, standing conspicuously among the best of their time. They strove by word and deed to save the color line from becoming the line between the bond and free, but all that they could do was nullified by Eli Whitney and the Curse of Gold. So they passed into forgetfulness.

But their spirit did not wholly die; here and there in the early part of the century came other exceptional men. Some were natural sons of unnatural fathers and were given often a liberal training and thus a race of educated mulattoes sprang up to plead for the black men's rights.

There was Ira Aldridge, whom all Europe loved to honor; there was that voice crying in the Wilderness, David Walker, and saying:

"I declare it does appear to me as though some nations think God is asleep, or that he made the Africans for nothing else but to dig their mines and work their farms, or they cannot believe history, sacred or profane. I ask every man who has a heart, and is blessed with the privilege of believing—Is not God a God of justice to all his creatures? Do you say he is? Then if he gives peace and tranquility to tyrants and permits them to keep our fathers, our mothers, ourselves and our children in eternal ignorance and wretchedness to support them and their families, would he be to us a God of Justice? I ask, O, ye Christians, who hold us and our children in the most abject ignorance and degradation that ever a people were afflicted with since the world began—I say if God gives you peace and tranquility, and suffers you thus to go on afflicting us, and our children, who have never given you the least provocation—would he be to us a God of Justice? If you will allow that we are men, who feel for each other, does not the blood of our fathers and of us, their children, cry aloud to the Lord of Sabaoth against you for the cruelties and murders with which you have and do continue to afflict us?"

This was the wild voice that first aroused Southern legislators in 1829 to the terrors of abolitionism.

In 1831 there met that first Negro convention in Philadelphia, at which the world gaped curiously but which bravely attacked the problems of race and slavery, crying out against persecution and declaring that "Laws as cruel in themselves as they were unconstitutional and unjust, have in many places been enacted against our poor, unfriended and unoffending brethren (without a shadow of provocation on our part), at whose bare recital the very savage draws himself up for fear of contagion—looks noble and prides himself because he bears not the name of Christian." Side by side this free Negro movement, and the movement for abolition, strove until they merged into one strong stream. Too little notice has been taken of the work which the Talented Tenth among Negroes took in the great abolition crusade. From the very day that a Philadelphia colored man became the first subscriber to Garrison's "Liberator," to the day when Negro soldiers made the Emancipation Proclamation possible, black leaders worked shoulder to shoulder with white men in a movement, the success of which would have been impossible without them. There was Purvis and Remond, Pennington and Highland Garnet, Sojourner Truth and Alexander Crummell, and above all, Frederick Douglass—what would the abolition movement have been without them? They stood as living examples of the possibilities of the Negro race, their own hard experiences and well-wrought culture said silently more than all the drawn periods of orators—they were the men who made American slavery impossible. As Maria Weston Chapman once said, from the school of anti-slavery agitation "a throng of authors, editors, lawyers, orators and accomplished gentlemen of color have taken their degree! It has equally implanted hopes and aspirations, noble thoughts, and sublime purposes, in the hearts of both races. It has prepared the white man for the freedom of the black man, and it has made the black man scorn the thought of enslavement, as does a white man, as far as its influence has extended. Strengthen that noble influence! Before its organization, the country only saw here and there in slavery some faithful Cudjoe or Dinah, whose strong natures blossomed even in bondage, like a fine plant beneath a heavy stone. Now, under the elevating and cherishing influence of the American Anti-slavery Society, the colored race, like the white, furnishes Corinthian capitals for the noblest temples."

Where were these black abolitionists trained? Some, like Frederick Douglass, were self-trained, but yet trained liberally; others like Alexander Crummell and McCune Smith, graduated from famous foreign universities. Most of them rose up through the colored schools of New York and Philadelphia and Boston, taught by college-bred men like Russworm, of Dartmouth, and college-bred white men like Neau and Benezet.

After emancipation came a new group of educated and gifted leaders: Langston, Bruce and Elliot, Greener, Williams and Payne. Through political organization, historical and polemic writing and moral regeneration, these men strove to uplift their people. It is now the fashion of to-day to sneer at them and to say that with freedom Negro leadership should have begun at the plow and not in the Senate—a foolish and mischievous lie; two hundred and fifty years that black serf toiled at the plow and yet that toiling was in vain till the Senate passed the war amendments; and two hundred and fifty years more the half-free serf of to-day may toil at his plow, but unless he have political rights and righteously guarded civic status, he will still remain the poverty-stricken and ignorant plaything of rascals, that he now is. This all sane men know even if they dare not say it.

And so now we come to the present—a day of cowardice and vacillation, of strident wide-voiced wrong and faint hearted compromise; of double-faced dallying with Truth and Right. Who are to-day guiding the work of the Negro people? The "exceptions" of course. And yet so sure as this Talented Tenth is pointed out, the blind worshippers of the Average cry out in alarm: "These are the exceptions, look here at death, disease and crime—these are the happy rule." Of course they are the rule, because a silly nation made them the rule: Because for three long centuries this people lynched Negroes who dared to be brave, raped black women who dared to be virtuous, crushed dark-hued youth who dared to be ambitious, and encouraged and made to flourish servility and lewdness and apathy. But not even this was able to crush all manhood and chastity and aspiration from black folk. A saving remnant continually survives and persists, continually aspires, continually shows itself in thrift and ability and character. Exceptional it is to be sure, but this is its chiefest promise; it shows the capability of Negro blood, the promise of black men. Do Americans ever stop to reflect that there are in this land a million men of Negro blood, well-educated, owners of homes, against the honor of whose womanhood no breath was ever raised, whose men occupy positions of trust and usefulness, and who, judged by any standard, have reached the full measure of the best type of modern European culture? Is it fair, is it decent, is it Christian to ignore these facts of the Negro problem, to belittle such aspiration, to nullify such leadership and seek to crush these people back into the mass out of which by toil and travail, they and their fathers have raised themselves?

Can the masses of the Negro people be in any possible way more quickly raised than by the effort and example of this aristocracy of talent and character? Was there ever a nation on God's fair earth civilized from the bottom upward? Never; it is, ever was and ever will be from the top downward that culture filters. The Talented Tenth rises and pulls all that are worth the saving up to their vantage ground. This is the history of human progress; and two historic mistakes which have hindered that progress were the thinking first that no more could ever rise save the few already risen; or second, that it would better the unrisen to pull the risen down.

How then shall the leaders of a struggling people be trained and the hands of the risen few be strengthened? There can be but one answer: The best and most capable of their youth must be schooled in the colleges and universities of the land. We will not quarrel as to just what the university of the Negro should teach or how it should teach it—I willingly admit that each soul and each race-soul needs its own peculiar curriculum. But this is true: A university is a human invention for the transmission of knowledge and culture from generation to generation, through the training of quick minds and pure hearts, and for this work no other human invention will suffice, not even trade and industrial schools.

All men cannot go to college but some men must; every isolated group or nation must have its yeast, must have for the talented few centers of training where men are not so mystified and befuddled by the hard necessary toil of earning a living, as to have no aims higher than their bellies, and no God greater than Gold. This is true training, and thus in the beginning were the favored sons of the freedmen trained. Out of the colleges of the North came, Cravath, Chase, Andrews, Bumstead and Spence to build the foundations of knowledge and civilization in the black South. Where ought they to have begun to build? At the bottom, of course, quibbles the mole with his eyes in the earth. Aye! truly at the bottom, at the very bottom; at the bottom of knowledge, down in the very depths of knowledge there where the roots of justice strike into the lowest soil of Truth. And so they did begin; they founded colleges, and up from the colleges shot normal schools, and out from the normal schools went teachers, and around the normal teachers clustered other teachers to teach the public schools; the colleges trained in Greek and Latin and mathematics, 2,000 men; and these men trained full 50,000 others in morals and manners and they in turn taught thrift and the alphabet to nine millions of men, who to-day hold $300,000,000 of property. It was a miracle—the most wonderful peace-battle of the nineteenth century, and yet to-day men smile at it, and in fine superiority tell us that it was all a strange mistake; that a proper way to found a system of education is first to gather the children and buy them spelling books and hoes; afterward men may look about for teachers, if haply they find them; or again they would teach men Work, but as for Life—why, what has Work to do with Life, they ask vacantly.

Was the work of these college founders successful; did it stand the test of time? Did the college graduates, with all their fine theories of life, really live? Are they useful men helping to civilize and elevate their less fortunate fellows? Let us see. Omitting all institutions which have not actually graduated students from college courses, there are to-day in the United States thirty-four institutions giving something above high school training to Negroes and designed especially for this race.

Three of these were established in the border States before the War; thirteen were planted by the Freedmen's Bureau in the years 1864–1869; nine were established between 1870 and 1880 by various church bodies; five were established after 1881 by Negro churches, and four are state institutions supported by United States' agricultural funds. In most cases the college departments are small adjuncts to high and common school work. As a matter of fact six institutions—Atlanta, Fisk, Howard, Shaw, Wilberforce and Leland, are the important Negro colleges so far as actual work and number of students are concerned. In all these institutions, seven hundred and fifty Negro college students are enrolled. In grade the best of these colleges are about a year behind the smaller New England colleges and a typical curriculum is that of Atlanta University. Here students from the grammar grades, after a three years' high school course, take a college course of 136 weeks. One-fourth of this time is given to Latin and Greek; one-fifth, to English and modern languages; one-sixth, to history and social science; one-seventh, to natural science; one-eighth to mathematics, and one-eighth to philosophy and pedagogy.

In addition to these students in the South, Negroes have attended Northern colleges for many years. As early as 1826 one was graduated from Bowdoin college, and from that time till to-day nearly every year has seen elsewhere, other such graduates. They have, of course, met much color prejudice. Fifty years ago very few colleges would admit them at all. Even to-day no Negro has ever been admitted to Princeton, and at some other leading institutions they are rather endured than encouraged. Oberlin was the great pioneer in the work of blotting out the color line in colleges, and has more Negro graduates by far than any other Northern college.

The total number of Negro college graduates up to 1899 (several of the graduates of that year not being reported), was as follows:

	NEGRO COLLEGES	WHITE COLLEGES
Before '76	137	75
'75–80	143	22
'80–85	250	31
'85–90	413	43
'90–95	465	66
'95–99	475	88
Class Unknown	57	64
TOTAL	1,940	389

Of these graduates 1,079 were men and 250 were women; 50 per cent of Northern-born college men come South to work among the masses of their people, at a sacrifice which few people realize; nearly 90 per cent of the Southern-born graduates instead of seeking that personal freedom and broader intellectual atmosphere which their training has led them, in some degree, to conceive, stay and labor and wait in the midst of their black neighbors and relatives.

The most interesting question, and in many respects the crucial question, to be asked concerning college-bred Negroes, is: Do they earn a living? It has been intimated more than once that the higher training of Negroes has resulted in sending into the world of work, men who could find nothing to do suitable to their talents. Now and then there comes a rumor of a colored college man working at menial service, etc. Fortunately, returns as to occupations of college-bred Negroes, gathered by the Atlanta conference, are quite full—nearly 60 per cent of the total number of graduates.

This enables us to reach fairly certain conclusions as to the occupations of all college-bred Negroes. Of 1,312 persons reported, there were:

	PER CENT	
Teachers,	53.4	xxxxxxxxxxxxxxxxxx
Clergymen,	16.8	xxxxxx
Physicians, etc.,	6.3	xxx
Students,	5.6	xx
Lawyers,	4.7	xx
In Govt. Service,	4.0	x
In Business,	3.6	x

PER CENT

Farmers and Artisans,	2.7	X
Editors, Secretaries and Clerks,	2.4	
Miscellaneous,	.5	

Over half are teachers, a sixth are preachers, another sixth are students and professional men; over 6 per cent are farmers, artisans and merchants, and 4 per cent are in government service. In detail the occupations are as follows:

OCCUPATIONS OF COLLEGE-BRED MEN

TEACHERS:

Presidents and Deans,	19		
Teachers of Music,	7		
Professors, Principals and Teachers,	675	Total	701

CLERGYMEN:

Bishop,	1		
Chaplains, U.S. Army,	2		
Missionaries,	9		
Presiding Elders,	12		
Preachers,	197	Total	221

PHYSICIANS:

Doctors of Medicine,	76		
Druggists,	4		
Dentists,	3	Total	83

STUDENTS,   74

LAWYERS,   62

CIVIL SERVICE:

U.S. Minister Plenipotentiary,	1
U.S. Consul,	1

OCCUPATIONS OF COLLEGE-BRED MEN

U.S. Deputy Collector,	1		
U.S. Gauger,	1		
U.S. Postmasters,	2		
U.S. Clerks,	44		
State Civil Service,	2		
City Civil Service,	1	Total	53
BUSINESS MEN:			
Merchants, etc.,	30		
Managers,	13		
Real Estate Dealers,	4	Total	47
FARMERS,			26
CLERKS AND SECRETARIES:			
Secretary of National Societies,	7		
Clerks, etc.,	15	Total	22
ARTISANS,			9
EDITORS,			9
MISCELLANEOUS,			5

These figures illustrate vividly the function of the college-bred Negro. He is, as he ought to be, the group leader, the man who sets the ideals of the community where he lives, directs its thoughts and heads its social movements. It need hardly be argued that the Negro people need social leadership more than most groups; that they have no traditions to fall back upon, no long established customs, no strong family ties, no well defined social classes. All these things must be slowly and painfully evolved. The preacher was, even before the war, the group leader of the Negroes, and the church their greatest social institution. Naturally this preacher was ignorant and often immoral, and the problem of replacing the older type by better educated men has been a difficult one. Both by direct work and by direct influence on other preachers, and on congregations, the college-bred preacher has an opportunity for reformatory work and moral inspiration, the value of which cannot be overestimated.

It has, however, been in the furnishing of teachers that the Negro college has found its peculiar function. Few persons realize how vast a work, how mighty a revolution has been thus accomplished. To furnish five millions and more of ignorant people with teachers of their own race and blood, in one generation, was not only a very difficult undertaking, but a very important one, in that, it placed before the eyes of almost every Negro child an attainable ideal. It brought the masses of the blacks in contact with modern civilization, made black men the leaders of their communities and trainers of the new generation. In this work college-bred Negroes were first teachers, and then teachers of teachers. And here it is that the broad culture of college work has been of peculiar value. Knowledge of life and its wider meaning, has been the point of the Negro's deepest ignorance, and the sending out of teachers whose training has not been simply for bread winning, but also for human culture, has been of inestimable value in the training of these men.

In the earlier years the two occupations of preacher and teacher were practically the only ones open to the black college graduate. Of later years a larger diversity of life among his people has opened new avenues of employment. Nor have these college men been paupers and spendthrifts; 557 college-bred Negroes owned in 1899, $1,342,862.50 worth of real estate (assessed value), or $2,411 per family. The real value of the total accumulations of the whole group is perhaps about $10,000,000, or $5,000 apiece.

Pitiful, is it not, beside the fortunes of oil kings and steel trusts, but after all is the fortune of the millionaire the only stamp of true and successful living? Alas! it is, with many, and there's the rub.

The problem of training the Negro is to-day immensely complicated by the fact that the whole question of the efficiency and appropriateness of our present systems of education, for any kind of child, is a matter of active debate, in which final settlement seems still afar off. Consequently it often happens that persons arguing for or against certain systems of education for Negroes have these controversies in mind and miss the real question at issue. The main question, so far as the Southern Negro is concerned, is: What under the present circumstance, must a system of education do in order to raise the Negro as quickly as possible in the scale of civilization? The answer to this question seems to me clear: It must strengthen the Negro's character, increase his knowledge and teach him to earn a living. Now it goes without saying, that it is hard to do all these things simultaneously or suddenly, and that at the same time it will not do to give all the attention to one and neglect the others; we could give black boys trades, but that alone will not civilize a race of ex-slaves; we might simply increase their knowledge of the world, but this would not necessarily make them wish to use this knowledge honestly; we might seek to strengthen character and purpose, but to what end if this people have nothing to eat or to wear? A system of education is not one thing, nor does it have a single definite object, nor is it a mere matter of schools. Education is that whole system of human training within and without the school house walls, which molds and develops men. If then we start out to train an ignorant and unskilled people with a heritage of bad habits, our system of training must set before itself two great aims—the one dealing with knowledge and character, the other part seeking to give the child the technical knowledge necessary for him to earn a living under the present circumstances. These objects are accomplished in part by the opening of the common schools on the one, and of the industrial schools on the other. But only in part, for there must also be trained those who are to teach these schools—men and women of knowledge and culture and technical skill who understand modern civilization, and having the training and aptitude to impart it to the children under them. There must be teachers, and teachers of teachers, and to attempt to establish any sort of system of common and industrial school training, without *first* (and I say *first* advisedly) without *first* providing for the higher training of the very best teachers, is simply throwing your money to the winds. School houses do not teach themselves—piles of brick and mortar and machinery do not send out *men*. It is the trained, living human soul, cultivated and strengthened by long study and thought, that breathes the real breath of life into boys and girls and makes them human, whether they be black or white, Greek, Russian or American. Nothing, in these latter days, has so dampened the faith of thinking Negroes in recent educational movements, as the fact that such movements have been accompanied by ridicule and denouncement and decrying of those very institutions of higher training which made the Negro public school possible, and make the Negro industrial schools thinkable. It was Fisk, Atlanta, Howard and Straight, those colleges born of the faith and sacrifice of the abolitionists, that placed in the black schools of the South 30,000 teachers and more, which some, who depreciate the work of these higher schools, are using to teach their own new experiments. If Hampton, Tuskegee and the hundred other industrial schools prove in the future to be as successful as they deserve to be, then their success in training black artisans for the South will be due primarily to the white colleges of the North and the black colleges of the South, which trained the teachers who to-day conduct these institutions. There was a time when the American people believed pretty devoutly that a log of wood with a boy at one end and Mark Hopkins at the other, represented the highest ideal of human training. But in these eager days it would seem that we have changed all that and think it necessary to add a couple of saw-mills and a hammer to this outfit, and, at a pinch, to dispense with the services of Mark Hopkins.

I would not deny, or for a moment seem to deny, the paramount necessity of teaching the Negro to work, and to work steadily and skillfully; or seem to depreciate in the slightest degree the important part industrial schools must play in the accomplishments of these ends, but I *do* say, and insist upon it, that it is industrialism drunk with its vision of success, to imagine that its own work can be accomplished without providing for the training of broadly cultured men and women to teach its own teachers, and to teach the teachers of the public schools.

But I have already said that human education is not simply a matter of schools; it is much more a matter of family and group life—the training of one's home, of one's daily companions, of one's social class. Now the black boy of the South moves in a black world—a world with its own leaders, its own thoughts, its own ideals. In this world he gets by far the larger part of his life training, and through the eyes of this dark world he peers into the veiled world beyond. Who guides and determines the education which he receives in his world? His teachers here are the group leaders of the Negro people—the physicians and clergymen, the trained fathers and mothers, the influential and forceful men about him of all kinds; here it is, if at all, that the culture of the surrounding world trickles through and is handed on by the graduates of the higher schools. Can such culture training of group-leaders be neglected? Can we afford to ignore it? Do you think that if the leaders of thought among Negroes are not trained and educated thinkers, that they will have no leaders? On the contrary a hundred half-trained demagogues will still hold the places they so largely occupy now, and hundreds of vociferous busy-bodies will multiply. You have no choice; either you must help furnish this race from within its own ranks with thoughtful men of trained leadership, or you must suffer the evil consequences of a headless misguided rabble.

I am an earnest advocate of manual training and trade teaching for black boys, and for white boys, too. I believe that next to the founding of Negro colleges the most valuable addition to Negro education since the war, has been industrial training for black boys. Nevertheless, I insist that the object of all true education is not to make men carpenters, it is to make carpenters men; there are two means of making the carpenter a man, each equally important: the first is to give the group and community in which he works, liberally trained teachers and leaders to teach him and his family what life means; the second is to give him sufficient intelligence and technical skill to make him an efficient workman; the first object demands the Negro college and college-bred men—not a quantity of such colleges, but a few of excellent quality; not too many college-bred men, but enough to leaven the lump, to inspire the masses, to raise the Talented Tenth to leadership; the second object demands a good system of common schools, well-taught, conveniently located and properly equipped.

The Sixth Atlanta Conference truly said in 1901:

"We call the attention of the Nation to the fact that less than one million of the three million Negro children of school age, are at present regularly attending school, and these attend a session which lasts only a few months.

"We are to-day deliberately rearing millions of our citizens in ignorance, and at the same time limiting the rights of citizenship by educational qualifications. This is unjust. Half the black youth of the land have no opportunities open to them for learning to read, write and cipher. In the discussion as to the proper training of Negro children after they leave the public schools, we have forgotten that they are not yet decently provided with public schools.

"Propositions are beginning to be made in the South to reduce the already meagre school facilities of Negroes. We congratulate the South on resisting, as much as it has, this pressure, and on the many millions it has spent on Negro education. But it is only fair to point out that Negro taxes and the Negroes' share of the income from indirect taxes and endowments have fully repaid this expenditure, so that the Negro public school system has not in all probability cost the white taxpayers a single cent since the war.

"This is not fair. Negro schools should be a public burden, since they are a public benefit. The Negro has a right to demand good common school training at the hands of the States and the Nation since by their fault he is not in position to pay for this himself."

What is the chief need for the building up of the Negro public school in the South? The Negro race in the South needs teachers to-day above all else. This is the current testimony of all who know the situation. For the supply of this great demand two things are needed—institutions of higher education and money for school houses and salaries. It is usually assumed that a hundred or more institutions for Negro training are to-day turning out so many teachers and college-bred men that the race is threatened with an over-supply. This is sheer nonsense. There are today less than 3,000 living Negro college graduates in the United States, and less than 1,000 Negroes in college. Moreover, in the 164 schools for Negroes, 95 per cent of their students are doing elementary and secondary work, work which should be done in the public schools. Over half of the remaining 2,157 students are taking high school studies. The mass of so-called "normal" schools for the Negro are simply doing elementary common school work, or, at most, high school work, with a little instruction in methods. The Negro colleges and the post-graduate courses at other institutions are the only agencies for the broader and more careful training of teachers. The work of these institutions is hampered for lack of funds. It is getting increasingly difficult to get funds for training teachers in the best modern methods, and yet all over the South, from State Superintendents, county officials, city boards and school principals comes the wail, "We need *teachers*!" and teachers must be trained. As the fairest minded of all white Southerners, Atticus G. Haygood, once said: "The defects of colored teachers are so great as to create an urgent necessity for training better ones. Their excellencies and their successes are sufficient to justify the best hopes of success in the effort, and to vindicate the judgment of those who make large investments of money and service, to give to colored students opportunity for thoroughly preparing themselves for the work of teaching children of their people."

The truth of this has been strikingly shown in the marked improvement of white teachers in the South. Twenty years ago the rank and file of white public school teachers were not as good as the Negro teachers. But they, by scholarships and good salaries, have been encouraged to thorough normal collegiate preparation, while the Negro teachers have been discouraged by starvation wages and the idea that any training will do for a black teacher. If carpenters are needed it is well and good to train men as carpenters. But to train men as carpenters, and then set them to teaching is wasteful and criminal; and to train men as teachers and then refuse them a living wage, unless they become carpenters, is rank nonsense.

The United States Commissioner of Education says in his report for 1900: "For comparison between the white and colored enrollment in secondary and higher education, I have added together the enrollment in high schools and secondary schools with the attendance in colleges and universities, not being sure of the actual grade of work done in the colleges and universities. The work done in the secondary schools is reported in such detail in this office, that there can be no doubt of its grade."

He then makes the following comparisons of persons in every million enrolled in secondary and higher education:

	WHOLE COUNTRY	NEGROES
1880	4,362	1,289
1900	10,743	2,061

And he concludes: "While the number in colored high schools and colleges had increased somewhat faster than the population, it had not kept pace with the average of the whole country, for it had fallen from 30 per cent to 24 per cent of the average quota. Of all colored pupils, one (1) in one hundred was engaged in secondary and higher work, and that ratio has continued substantially for the past twenty years. If the ratio of colored population in secondary and higher education is to be equal to the average for the whole country, it must be increased to five times its present average." And if this be true of the secondary and higher education, it is safe to say that the Negro has not one-tenth his quota in college studies. How baseless, therefore, is the charge of too much training! We need Negro teachers for the Negro common schools, and we need first-class normal schools and colleges to train them. This is the work of higher Negro education and it must be done.

Further than this, after being provided with group leaders of civilization, and a foundation of intelligence in the public schools, the carpenter, in order to be a man, needs technical skill. This calls for trade school. Now trade schools are not nearly such simple things as people once thought. The original idea was that the "Industrial" school was to furnish education, practically free, to those willing to work for it; it was to "do" things—i.e.: become a center of productive industry, it was to be partially, if not wholly, self-supporting, and it was to teach trades. Admirable as were some of the ideas underlying this scheme, the whole thing simply would not work in practice; it was found that if you were to use time and material to teach trades thoroughly, you could not at the same time keep the industries on a commercial basis and make them pay. Many schools started out to do this on a large scale and went into virtual bankruptcy. Moreover, it was found also that it was possible to teach a boy a trade mechanically, without giving him the full educative benefit of the process, and, vice versa, that there was a distinctive educative value in teaching a boy to use his hands and eyes in carrying out certain physical processes, even though he did not actually learn a trade. It has happened, therefore, in the last decade that a noticeable change has come over the industrial schools. In the first place the idea of commercially remunerative industry in a school is being pushed rapidly to the background. There are still schools with shops and farms that bring in an income, and schools that use student labor partially for the erection of their buildings and the furnishing of equipment. It is coming to be seen, however, in the education of the Negro, as clearly as it has been seen in the education of the youths the world over, that it is the *boy* and not the material product, that is the true object of education. Consequently the object of the industrial school came to be the thorough training of boys regardless of the cost of the training, so long as it was thoroughly well done.

Even at this point, however, the difficulties were not surmounted. In the first place modern industry has taken great strides since the war, and the teaching of trades is no longer a simple matter. Machinery and the long processes of work have greatly changed the work of the carpenter, the iron worker and the shoemaker. A really efficient workman must be to-day an intelligent man who has had good technical training in addition to thorough common school, and perhaps even higher training. To meet this situation the industrial schools began a further development; they established distinct Trade Schools for the thorough training of better class artisans, and at the same time they sought to preserve for the purpose of general education, such of the simpler processes of the elementary trade learning as were best suited therefor. In this differentiation of the Trade School and manual training, the best of the industrial schools simply followed the plain trend of the present educational epoch. A prominent educator tells us that, in Sweden, "In the beginning the economic conception was generally adopted, and everywhere manual training was looked upon as a means of preparing the children of the common people to earn their living. But gradually it came to be recognized that manual training has a more elevated purpose, and one, indeed, more useful in the deeper meaning of the term. It came to be considered as an educative process for the complete moral, physical and intellectual development of the child."

Thus, again, in the manning of trade schools and manual training schools we are thrown back upon the higher training as its source and chief support. There was a time when any aged and worn-out carpenter could teach in a trade school. But not so to-day. Indeed the demand for college-bred men by a school like Tuskegee ought to make Mr. Booker T. Washington the firmest friend of higher training. Here he has as helpers the son of a Negro senator, trained in Greek and the humanities, and graduated at Harvard; the son of a Negro congressman and lawyer, trained in Latin and mathematics, and graduated at Oberlin; he has as his wife, a woman who read Virgil and Homer in the same class room with me; he has as college chaplain, a classical graduate of Atlanta University; as teacher of science, a graduate of Fisk; as teacher of history, a graduate of Smith—indeed some thirty of his chief teachers are college graduates, and instead of studying French grammars in the midst of weeds, or buying pianos for dirty cabins, they are at Mr. Washington's right hand helping him in a noble work. And yet one of the effects of Mr. Washington's propaganda has been to throw doubt upon the expediency of such training for Negroes, as these persons have had.

Men of America, the problem is plain before you. Here is a race transplanted through the criminal foolishness of your fathers. Whether you like it or not the millions are here, and here they will remain. If you do not lift them up, they will pull you down. Education and work are the levers to uplift a people. Work will not do it unless inspired by the right ideals and guided by intelligence. Education must not simply teach work—it must teach life. The Talented Tenth of the Negro race must be made leaders of thought and missionaries of culture among their people. No others can do this work and the Negro colleges must train men for it. The Negro race, like all other races, is going to be saved by its exceptional men.

"The Talented Tenth Memorial Address"
W. E. B. Du Bois

*(delivered at the Nineteenth Grand Boulé Conclave,
Sigma Pi Phi, 1948)*

THE PAST

SOME YEARS ago I used the phrase "The Talented Tenth," meaning leadership of the Negro race in America by a trained few. Since then this idea has been criticized. It has been said that I had in mind the building of an aristocracy with neglect of the masses. This criticism has seemed even more valid because of emphasis on the meaning and power of the mass of people to which Karl Marx gave voice in the middle of the nineteenth century, and which has been growing in influence ever since. There have come other changes in these days, which a great many of us do not realize as Revolution through which we are passing. Because of this, it is necessary to examine the world about us and our thoughts and attitudes toward it. I want then to re-examine and restate the thesis of the Talented Tenth which I laid down many years ago.

In a day when culture is comparatively static, a man once grounded in the fundamentals of knowledge, received through current education, can depend on the more or less routine absorption of knowledge for keeping up with the world. This was true for decades during the nineteenth century, and usually has been true in the slow drift of many other centuries. But today, the tide runs swiftly, and almost every fundamental concept which most of us learned in college has undergone radical change; so that a man who was broadly educated in 1900 may be widely ignorant in 1948, unless he has made conscious, continuous, and determined effort to keep abreast with the development of knowledge and of thought in the last half century.

For instance, since 1900 physics and chemistry have been revolutionized in many of their basic concepts. Astronomy is today almost a new science as compared with the time of Copernicus. Psychology has risen from guesswork and introspection to an exact science. Biology and anthropology have changed and expanded widely; and history and sociology have begun in the middle of the twentieth century, first, to take on the shape of real sciences rather than being largely theory and opinion.

If, now, a college man of 1900, or even of 1925, has spent his time since graduation mainly in making a living, he is in fair way not to be able to understand the world of 1950. It is necessary then for men of education continually to readjust their knowledge, and this is doubly necessary in this day of swift revolution in ideas, in ideals, in industrial techniques, in rapid travel, and in varieties and kinds of human contacts.

Turn now to that complex of social problems, which surrounds and conditions our life, and which we call more or less vaguely, the Negro Problem. It is clear that in 1900, American Negroes were an inferior caste, were frequently lynched and mobbed, widely disfranchised, and usually segregated in the main areas of life. As student and worker at that time, I looked upon them and saw salvation through intelligent leadership; as I said, through a "Talented Tenth." And for this intelligence, I argued, we needed college-trained men. Therefore, I stressed college and higher training. For these men with their college training, there would be needed thorough understanding of the mass of Negroes and their problems; and, therefore, I emphasized scientific study. Willingness to work and make personal sacrifice for solving these problems was of course, the first prerequisite and *Sine Qua Non*. I did not stress this, I assumed it.

SACRIFICE

I ASSUMED that with knowledge, sacrifice would automatically follow. In my youth and idealism, I did not realize that selfishness is even more natural than sacrifice. I made the assumption of its wide availability because of the spirit of sacrifice learned in my mission school training.

I went South to Fisk University at the age of 17, when I was peculiarly impressionable, from a region which had opened my mind but had not filled the void. At Fisk I met a group of teachers who would be unusual in any time or place. They were not only men of learning and experience, but men and women of character and almost fanatic devotion. It was a great experience to sit under their voice and influence. It was from that experience that I assumed easily that educated people, in most cases were going out into life to see how far they could better the world. Of course, as I looked about me, I might have understood, that all students of Fisk University were not persons of this sort. There was no lack of small and selfish souls; there were among the student body, careless and lazy fellows; and there were especially sharp young persons, who received the education given very cheaply at Fisk University, with the distinct and single-minded idea, of seeing how much they could make out of it for themselves, and nobody else.

When I came out of college into the world of work, I realized that it was quite possible that my plan of training a talented tenth might put in control and power, a group of selfish, self-indulgent, well-to-do men, whose basic interest in solving the Negro Problem was personal; personal freedom and unhampered enjoyment and use of the world, without any real care, or certainly no arousing care, as to what became of the mass of American Negroes, or of the mass of any people. My Talented Tenth, I could see, might result in a sort of interracial free-for-all, with the devil taking the hindmost and the foremost taking anything they could lay hands on.

ARISTOCRACY

THIS, HISTORICALLY, has always been the danger of aristocracy. It was for a long time regarded as almost inevitable because of the scarcity of ability among men and because, naturally the artistocrat came to regard himself and his whims as necessarily the end and only end of civilization and culture. As long as the masses supported this doctrine, aristocracy and mass misery lived amiably together.

Into this situation, came the revolutionary thought, first voiced in former ages by great moral leaders, which asked charity for the poor and sympathy for the ignorant and sick. And even intimated eventual justice in Heaven. But in the suddenly expanding economy and marvelous technique of the eighteenth and nineteenth centuries, there came prophets and reformers, but especially the voice of Karl Marx, to say that the poor need not always be with us, and that all men could and should be free from poverty.

Karl Marx stressed the fact that not merely the upper class but the mass of men were the real people of the world.

He insisted that the masses were poor, ignorant, and sick, not by sin or by nature but by oppression. He preached that planned production of goods and just distribution of income would abolish poverty, ignorance and disease, and make the so-called upper-class, not the exception, but the rule among mankind. He declared that the world was not for the few, but for the many; that out of the masses of men could come overwhelming floods of ability and genius, if we freed men by plan and not by rare chance. Civilization not only could be shared by the vast majority of men, but such civilization founded on a wide human base would be better and more enduring than anything that the world has seen. The world would thus escape the enduring danger of being run by a selfish few for their own advantage.

Very gradually as the philosophy of Karl Marx and many of his successors seeped into my understanding, I tried to apply this doctrine with regard to Negroes. My Talented Tenth must be more than talented, and work not simply as individuals. Its passport to leadership was not alone learning, but expert knowledge of modern economics as it affected American Negroes; and in addition to this and fundamental, would be its willingness to sacrifice and plan for such economic revolution in industry and just distribution of wealth, as would make the rise of our group possible.

RACE

MOREOVER, biology and sociology were reconstructing my idea of race. This group was not simply a physical entity: a black people, or a people descended from black folk. It was, what all races really are, a cultural group. It is too bad that we have to use the word "cultural" for so many meanings. But what it means in modern scientific thought is that 15,000,000 men and women who for three centuries have shared common experiences and common suffering, and have worked all those days and nights together for their own survival and progress; that this complex of habits and manners could not and must not be lost. That persons sharing this experience formed a race no matter what their blood may be. That this race must be conserved for the benefit of the Negro people themselves and for mankind. I came then to advocate, not pride of biological race, but pride in a cultural group, integrated and expanded by developed ideals, so as to form a method of progress.

Immediately this posed a paradox. Those Negroes who had long trained themselves for personal success and individual freedom, were coming to regard the disappearance of segregation as an end and not a means. They wanted to be Americans, and they did not care so much what kind of folk Americans were, as for the right to be one of them. They, not only, did not want to fight for a Negro culture, they even denied the possibility of any such animal, certainly its desirability even if it could be made to exist. The leadership, then, of my Talented Tenth over the mass of young colored men and women, college-trained and entering their careers, faced rejection and disappearance of the Negro, both as a race and as a culture.

But this, as I have said, was paradoxical. The United States has a large number of Negroes. We number as many as the inhabitants of the Argentine or of Czechoslovakia; or the whole of Scandinavia, including Sweden, Norway, and Denmark. We are very nearly the size of Egypt, Rumania and Yugoslavia. And we are larger than Canada, Saudi Arabia, Ethiopia, Hungary, or the Netherlands. We have twice as many persons as Australia or Switzerland, and more than the whole Union of South Africa. We have more people than Portugal or Peru; twice as many as Greece and nearly as many as Turkey. We have more people by far than Belgium, and half as many as Spain.

A nation of such size, such history, such accomplishment, should be able to look forward to something more than complete effacement and utter absorption in another and foreign entity. It should have legitimate dreams of continuity, unity, and immortality. It should plan a life and future, not in world antagonism and enmity, or narrow racial provincialism, but in higher and broader helpfulness to all, through self-knowledge, self-realization, and self-control. Not only that, but the world has at least 250,000,000 Negroes and Negroids. They cannot disappear physically, much less culturally, without deep loss to themselves and humanity.

NEGRO CULTURE

THE QUESTION IS: how and by whom can Negro culture be preserved? Not simply for the social movements of America, but for the greater world of human culture.

In our concentration of thought on the United States, as the locus of our fight, we have come to think of this land as the center of the universe and lately as the predestined leader of civilization. This is because of our recent growth in world power, based on unusual natural resources; a democracy in government which emancipated former lower classes, and gave them work and high wages; and finally, because the leading nations of Europe lost their power through rivalry, exploitation, and war.

It was not America's virtues, but Europe's mistakes, that gave us our present primacy. We Negroes have thoughtlessly failed to recognize this and have tried to become more American than the Americans; loud in our conversation, our boasting and arrogance, showy and ostentatious in dress, careless in manners, wasteful in conspicuous expenditure, and smug and uncritical in judgment. Like all America we read few books; we get superficial "news" from radio gossip and doctored opinion from a press known to be prejudiced and monopolized. We do not realize, that today the United States is probably the most thoroughly hated and despised nation on earth, especially among the really cultured and civilized. Its natural resources, industrial techniques, and control of credit make it powerful and feared; but it is not recognized as leading in science, in morals, or toward human happiness. The remaking of human culture, so as to fashion a decent world, is being pursued today mainly in Europe and Asia.

Cooperation then, with the forward-looking forces of civilization in the world, can be carried out in this land by Negroes, quite as well as by any other large coherent American group. This is recognized in foreign thought. It is becoming a matter of open expression among hundreds of millions of people in Africa and in Asia. These people are not, as we usually assume when we unconsciously take over American prejudices, people who deserve to be ignored, in our estimate of the world and in our dreams of what the world may be. Not only have they been influential in their contributions to the past, but today, there is a leadership from the colored world which is beginning to be powerful on earth.

ECONOMIC RECONSTRUCTION

NOW THE central thought of any cultural effort to restore the civilization which has collapsed in two world wars, and to build something better is economic reconstruction. Ignorance of this central fact is widespread. Economics is not being taught as it should be in the schools and colleges today: and I mean of course by economics—knowledge of the meaning of work, of how it may best be done; of the significance and ownership of machines, of the role of credit and money; of the distribution of goods and services, of the possibilities of human effort today.

The new economics starting almost exactly a hundred years ago is clear and unanswerable in its facts and knowledge. It says that nature is the source of all wealth: that human effort transforms natural resources for human use: that the results of this work should be divided among men according to need and not by chance, or privilege or by individual power. It says that industry should be controlled by the state, and planned by science and that all goods should be owned and distributed in such ways as result in the greatest good to all. All persons should be educated according to ability and should labor according to efficiency. Health and housing, social security, facilities for recreation and for human intercourse should be public responsibilities.

Within this framework of necessary work for general welfare there should be the widest possible area reserved for liberty of thought and of action and for creative ideas.

This program of progress is the consensus of the civilized world today. It is called by many names: Socialism, Communism, Liberalism, named according to place and time and emphasis.

In the United States, this idea has made wide progress beginning with the populist movement, progressing with Bryan and LaFollette and culminating with the New Deal under Franklin Roosevelt. But it has been steadily and often successfully opposed by industrial interests, which have tried desperately to make Americans turn back to the belief of the eighteenth and nineteenth centuries, that free individual enterprise, with the least possible social control and spurred mainly by the incentive of private profit, is the only method which can bring and preserve prosperity. This doctrine is contradicted by two world wars and the imminence of a third. It is denied in our own history by six industrial crises, a great depression which threw world industry into chaos, and threat of another tomorrow.

Yet triumphant reaction spurred by fantastic war profit is forcing the United States, against the consensus of the best opinion in the world, to block real economic progress by misdirecting knowledge through a monopolized and commercialized press and by a series of witch-hunts to scare and silence thought. This is a day of critical danger to us and to the world. Whatever we can do to avert disaster, is our bounden duty to attempt.

A NEW TALENTED TENTH

THE QUESTION is then: Who can lead the way in this effort? Here comes a new idea for a Talented Tenth: The concept of a group-leadership, not simply educated and self-sacrificing, but with clear vision of present world conditions and dangers, and conducting American Negroes to alliance with culture groups in Europe, America, Asia and Africa, and looking toward a new world culture. We can do it. We have the ability. The only question is, have we the will?

This calls for leadership through special organization. Such organization calls for more than a tenth of our number. One one-hundredth, or thirty thousand persons is indicated, with a directing council composed of educated and specially trained experts in the main branches of science and the main categories of human work, and a paid executive committee of five or six persons to carry out the program.

To launch so large a scheme as a new organization, would call for so much time, money and effort, that it would be more practical if an already existing body could be adapted to this work. Some of our secret fraternal orders might do it. The college fraternities would occur to all as best placed by education to inaugurate this work, if they could be persuaded of its necessity and feasibility. The under-graduate fraternities, even with their graduate chapters, have probably a constituency too young and too busy trying to make a living. Then, too, they are dominated by rather youthful ideals of the mis-called "college spirit." I turn then to this fraternity but with some misgiving. What the guiding idea of Sigma Pi Phi was, I have never been able to learn. I believe it was rooted in a certain exclusiveness and snobbery, for which we all have a yearning, even if unconfessed. But such an object belongs to days of peace and security. Today is a time of crisis. Could then, this organization be adapted to the role of organized scientific leadership of the American Negro?

SIGMA PI PHI

WE CONSIST of 440 families (omitting the Boulé of Baltimore from whom repeated letters and cards, airmailed and special delivered have elicited no response). Of 3,000,000 Negro families, we represent not a tenth, but a ten-thousandth of the group.

First of all, we are old men. Only one is under thirty: three-fourths of the Archons are between 30 and 60, and most probably nearer 60. More than a fourth are over 60. This means that by and large we received our college education in the last century or the first decade of this, when the atom was indivisible: when light always spread in straight lines: when evolution was the survival of the fittest: when mankind consisted of five separate, indestructible races and when socialism was a fool's dream.

In occupation our membership is not well-balanced. Nearly half (201) are physicians, dentists, and pharmacists. They are thus members of closed trade unions with rules coming down from another century: with highly individualized activities and restricted public contracts. The next group (144 in number) are teachers and administrators of schools, ministers and social workers. These men are more in touch with the new science and social movements, but have little first-hand experience in modern industry: that is, in the very activity which is ruling and conditioning the modern world.

A further group of 65 persons consists of lawyers and business men. They not only themselves have limited contact with the laboring classes and their problems, but are over-exposed to American business philosophy—to the idea of industry primarily for profit, of trade unions as nuisances and of high wages as inflationary. This comes from their contact with white fellow men in their professions, who are nearly all of the reactionary group. The remaining 30 members are varied in occupation but do not fill the clear vacancy which we have so far as authors and artists are concerned. We have 9 technicians but that is a very small number.

We do not represent then typical America. Nor do we represent at all the scientific and social leadership of the modern world, because we are overloaded with members of the professions, weighted towards American business, while science and art despite our teachers fall far behind. We are then in the mass, an old, timid, conservative group.

We are not, according to American standards, rich: but according to world standards, we are distinctly well-to-do and in the upper economic brackets. Of our membership, 127 receive over $10,000 a year and almost a score of these get over $25,000. There are 199 families who receive from $5,000 to $10,000 a year and only 86 who confess to less than $5,000, which may be modesty. Our interests then are not normally with the poor and hungry, yet we are not aware of this: we assume on the one hand our identity with the poor and yet we act and sympathize with the rich, an unconscious and dangerous dichotomy.

It is a matter of sorrow or congratulations, according to one's point of view, when we remember that this group is probably bound for extinction. Of the families, 159 have no children, and 88 only one child: three-fourths of the families have no grandchildren, and 39 only one grandchild. Our other 72 members may, barring accidents, partly reproduce our number, but at present there are only 243 grandchildren; when survival would call for 880!

Theoretically then this is not an ideal group for the kind of leadership which I have in mind. Moreover, it faces peculiar trends and difficulties. May I name six of these: first, a distinct indisposition to re-examine trends and knowledge or to question conclusions of the past. Second, a disposition to accept the values and decisions of present-day America. Third, a deep-seated disbelief in Asia and Africa and even of the West Indies, springing partially from the prejudice of surrounding Americans: partially from the idea that we, ourselves, are unusual and exceptional colored folk. Fourth, a feeling of helplessness against too great odds and tendencies: if the white world is going along an accepted path even if that is suicide, after all, what can we do about it, and what do we want to do about it? Fifth, a current philosophy among us as old as humanity, "eat, drink, and be merry"—a reaction towards throwing off of the extreme depression of the days when we were fighting for sheer existence and determination to enjoy some of the possibilities which our income and new freedom open to us today.

And finally in spite of some of the extraordinary things which we have seen Negroes do in the last generation in America, there still lingers among us the deep-seated doubt of Negro ability to cope with the white world. We are so painfully aware of the degradation of millions of our masses; of the crime and lechery that lurk in New York, Chicago and New Orleans; of the lying, dishonesty, and double dealing that mark so many even of our intelligent and rich, that we associate color and degradation and cannot make ourselves believe in any real triumph of black folk. Few of us know or try to know what human degradation on this earth can be and has been and is among other and fairer peoples.

Basically this confronts us with two problems: the leadership of the masses and the sacrifice necessary to leadership. The uplift of the mass cannot be left to chance. Marx and Lenin firmly believed it could only be accomplished by a dictatorship. I think in the case of Russia they were right; but in our plight, I think we can free our own mass by organization and group influence exercised through a self-sacrificing leadership. This is primarily a question of character which I failed to emphasize in my first proposal of a Talented Tenth.

CHARACTER

In this reorientation of my ideas, my pointing out the new knowledge necessary for leadership, and new ideas of race and culture, there still remains that fundamental and basic requirement of character for any successful leadership toward great ideals. Even if the ideals are clearly perceived, honesty of character and purity of motive is needed without which no effort succeeds or deserves to succeed. We used to talk much of character—perhaps too much. At Fisk, we had it dinned into our ears. At Harvard we never mentioned it. We thought of it: but it was not good taste to talk of it: At Berlin we quite forgot it. But that was reaction. We cannot have perfection. We have few saints. But we must have honest men or we die. We must have unselfish, far-seeing leadership or we fail.

What can Sigma Pi Phi do to see that we get it for the American Negro? So far as the group before me is concerned little can be done, for the simple reason that most of our present membership will soon be dead. Unless we begin to recruit this fraternity membership with young men and large numbers of them, our biennial conclaves will be increasingly devoted to obituaries. We should have a large increase of membership, drawn from men who have received their college education since the First World War. This new membership must not simply be successful in the American sense of being rich; they must not all be physicians and lawyers. The technicians, business men, teachers and social workers admitted must be those who realize the economic revolution now sweeping the world, and do not think that private profit is the measure of public welfare. And too: we must deliberately seek honest men.

This screened young membership must be far greater in

number than it is now. Baltimore for instance has more than 166,000 Negroes and only 23 in its Boulé, representing less than 100 persons. Surely there must be at least 23 other persons in Baltimore worthy of fellowship. It is inconceivable that we should even for a moment dream that with a membership of 440 we have scratched even the tip of the top of the surface of a group representative of potential Negro leadership in America. Nothing but congenital laziness should keep us from a membership of 3,000 by the next biennium without any lowering of quality; and a membership of 30,000 by 1960. This would be an actual numerical one hundredth of our race: a body large enough really to represent all. Yet small enough to insure exceptional quality; if screened for intelligent and disinterested planning.

A PLANNED PROGRAM

HAVING gotten a group of predominantly active virile men of middle age and settled opinions, who have finished their education and begun their life work, what can they do? They must first of all recognize the fact that their own place in life is primarily a matter of opportunity, rather than simply desert or ability. That if such opportunity were extended and broadened, a thousand times as many Negroes could join the ranks of the educated and able, instead of sinking into poverty, disease and crime; that the primary duty of this organization would be to find desert, ability, and character among young Negroes and get for them education and opportunity; that the major opportunity should be seen as work according to gift and training with pay sufficient to furnish a decent standard of living.

A national organization of this sort must be prepared to use propaganda, make investigation, plan procedures and even finance projects. This will call for an initial body of belief which even now can be forecast in outline.

We would want to impress on the emerging generations of Negroes in America, the ideal of plain living and high thinking, in defiance of American noise, waste and display; the rehabilitation of the indispensable family group, by deliberate planning of marriages, with mates selected for heredity, physique, health and brains, with less insistence on color, comeliness or romantic sex lure, mis-called love; youth should marry young and have a limited number of healthy children; the home must be a place of education, rather than cleaning and cooking, with books, discussion and entertainment.

The schools where these children are sent must not be chosen for the color of their teachers or students, but for their efficiency in educating a particular child. In home and out children should learn not to neglect our art heritage: music is not designed solely for night clubs; drama is not aimed at Broadway; dancing is not the handmaid of prostitution; and writing is not mainly for income.

Our religion with all of its dogma, demagoguery, and showmanship, can be a center to teach character, right conduct and sacrifice. There lies here a career for a Negro Gandhi and a host of earnest followers.

The dark hosts of Liberia and Ethiopia and other parts of Africa together with Asia, the Pacific lands, South and Central America, and the Caribbean area, have need for that broad knowledge of the world and special training in technique which we might learn and take to them. They do not need us for exploitation and get-rich-quick schemes. There is no reason why the sort of thought and teaching which 2,000 years ago made the groves of Athens the center of the world's salvation, could not live again in ten thousand Negro homes in America today.

Occupation should not, and need not, be left to chance or confined to what whites are doing, or are willing to let us do. It must involve innovation and experiment. It must be carefully planned, thoroughly thought-out with wide study of human wants, technical power, trained effort and consecrated devotion with the use of every scientific procedure in physics, chemistry, biology, psychology, sociology and history.

For this central object of planned work, this organization should assemble the best knowledge and experience. It should encourage pioneering and adventure; attacking desert places with modern technique; producing new goods by new processes; avoiding the factory system and mass production as the last word in work, and returning to the ideal of personal consumption, personal taste and human desire; thinking of consumption and the consumers as coming before production, and not of production as the end of industry and profit as its motive.

The new generation must learn that the object of the world is not profit but service and happiness. They must therefore be directed away from careers which are antisocial and dishonest, but immensely profitable. Insurance can be a social help but much of it today is organized theft. We must have drug stores, but the patent nostrums in which so many of them deal deserve the penitentiary. Gambling not only as poker-playing but as a profitable career, is seeping through all kinds of American business from the stock market, factory and wholesale store, to the numbers racket, horse racing, and radio gifts. Every effort should be made to warn the next generation away from this dry rot of death and crime.

An organization adapted to such a program of propaganda and work of guidance, and able to search for and select ability and character and finance efforts to give it opportunity, will need large funds at its disposal. The sacrifice necessary to provide such funds should be regarded not as sentimental charity or mushy religious fervor but as foresight and investment in the future of the Negro in America, and canny insurance against loss by wholesale neglect of invaluable human resources. We may reach the high ideal when again the tithe, the tenth of our income will go to the perfectly feasible effort of so civilizing the American Negro that he will be able to lead the world and will want to do so.

THE GUIDING HUNDREDTH

THIS, THEN, is my re-examined and restated theory of the "Talented Tenth," which has thus become the doctrine of the "Guiding Hundredth."

Naturally, I do not dream, that a word of mine will transform, to any essential degree, the form and trends of this fraternity; but I am certain the idea called for expression and that the seed must be dropped, whether in this or other soil, today or tomorrow.

NOTES

Preface

1. Hugh Price, from a speech delivered at the National Leadership Summit Meeting, November 17, 1995.

Parable of the Talents

I have discussed many of the ideas in this essay with Anthony Appiah, John Kain, Cornel West, and William Julius Wilson. Some of the material appeared in different form in *Forbes, Time,* and *The New Yorker;* in addition, I drew on descriptions of my Yale experiences from an essay I wrote in the 1960s for an anthology called *Hurdles,* edited by Herbert Sacks, M.D. (Atheneum).

1. Martin Luther King, Jr., *Where Do We Go from Here?* (Boston: Beacon Press, 1989), pp. 131–32; Harold Cruse, *Plural but Equal* (New York: William Morrow, 1987).
2. Jennifer L. Hochschild, *Facing Up to the American Dream: Race, Class, and the Soul of the Nation* (Princeton: Princeton University Press, 1995).
3. Ibid., p. 79.
4. For a dissenting view, see Adolph Reed, "Race and the Disruption of the New Deal Coalition," *Urban Affairs Quarterly* 27, no. 2 (December 1991): 326–33.
5. John Kain, "Housing Segregation, Negro Employment, and Metropolitan Decentralization," *Quarterly Journal of Economics* 82 (1968): 175–97; John D. Karsarda, "Urban Change and Minority Opportunities," in P. E. Peterson, ed., *The New Urban Reality* (Washington, D.C.: Brookings Institution, 1985), pp. 33–68.
6. Douglass Massey and Nancy A. Denton, "Trends in the

Residential Segregation of Blacks, Hispanics, and Asians: 1970–1980," *American Sociological Review* 52, no. 6: 785–801.

7. Barry Bluestone and Bennett Harrison, *The De-Industrialization of America: Plant Closings, Community Abandonment, and the Dismantling of Basic Industry* (New York: Basic Books, 1982). For an argument that, in fact, blacks were never well represented in the industrial sector, see Norman Fainstein, "The Underclass/Mismatch Hypothesis as an Explanation for Black Economic Deprivation," *Politics and Society* 15, no. 4 (1986–87): 439.

8. Christopher Jencks, *Rethinking Social Policy: Race, Poverty, and the Underclass* (Cambridge: Harvard University Press, 1992), p. 124.

9. Herbert J. Gans, *The War Against the Poor: The Underclass and Antipoverty Policy* (New York: Basic Books, 1995), pp. 117–18.

10. Joel F. Handler, *The Poverty of Welfare Reform* (New Haven: Yale University Press, 1995), p. 141.

11. Mark Lowery, "The Rise of the Black Professional Class," *Black Enterprise*, August 1995, p. 29.

12. Gary Orfield and Carole Ashkinaze, *The Closing Door* (Chicago: University of Chicago Press, 1991), p. 4.

13. "Precisely because the new black middle class is largely a product of government policy, its future is subject to the vagaries of politics," Stephen Steinberg argues in his *Turning Back: The Retreat from Racial Justice in American Thought and Policy* (Boston: Beacon Press, 1995), p. 198.

Black Strivings in a Twilight Civilization

1. This phrase comes from the first line of Muriel Rukeyser's "Poem"—"I lived in the first century of world wars"—in her book *The Speed of Darkness* (1968), in *A Muriel Rukeyser Reader*, ed. Jan Heller Levi (New York: W. W. Norton & Son, 1994), p. 211. In his magisterial treatment of this most violent of centuries, *The Age of Extremes: A History of the World, 1914–*

1991 (New York: Pantheon, 1994), Eric Hobsbawm suggests the numbers of this century's "Megadeath" toll to be 187 million (p. 12). Here he follows the estimate of Z. Brzezinski in *Out of Control: Global Turmoil on the Eve of the Twenty-First Century* (New York: Scribner, 1993). I think both scholars underestimate the death toll in this "most terrible century in Western history" (Isaiah Berlin's phrase).

2. In *Dusk of Dawn: An Essay Toward an Autobiography of a Race Concept* (1940), W. E. B. Du Bois writes, "Whatever of racial feeling gradually crept into my life, its effect upon me in these earlier days was rather one of exaltation and high disdain. . . . [M]y African racial feeling was then purely a matter of my own later learning and reaction. . . ." In W. E. B. Du Bois, *Writings* (New York: Library of America, 1986), pp. 563, 638. See also Eric J. Sundquist, *To Wake the Nations: Race in the Making of American Literature* (Cambridge: Harvard University Press, 1993), pp. 459–67; David Levering Lewis, *W. E. B. Du Bois: Biography of a Race, 1868–1919* (New York: Henry Holt & Co., 1993), pp. 56–70; and Manning Marable, *W. E. B. Du Bois: Black Radical Democrat* (Boston: Twayne Publishers, 1986), pp. 5–15.

3. W. E. B. Du Bois, "The Talented Tenth," in *Writings*, p. 852. As Peter Gay rightly notes, "The question of the lower orders is the great unexamined political question of the Enlightenment. . . . [In the writings of the *philosophes* there is] snobbery . . . [there is] a certain failure of imagination . . . [and there is] a sense of despair at the general wretchedness, illiteracy, and brutishness of the poor." *The Enlightenment: An Interpretation* (New York: Norton Library, 1969), vol. 2, *The Science of Freedom*, p. 517.

4. W. E. B. Du Bois, *The Souls of Black Folk* (New York: Fawcett Publications, 1961), pp. 48, 50, 75, 76, 83, 87, 101, 107, 109, 125, 126, 132, 139, 150, 170, 171, 182, 189. The last quote is from page 80.

5. Ibid., pp. 140–41.

6. In a brilliant essay, Shamoon Zamir makes a similar point about Du Bois. "As Du Bois details his curiosity and excitement

at the novelty of the situation, his posture is very much that of an ethnographic participant-observer reporting from the field. . . . [T]he feelings of the young Du Bois reproduce the same exoticism that led the white middle-class reading public at the turn of the century to seek out works that revealed how 'the other half' lived." Zamir grounds Du Bois's worldview in *The Souls of Black Folk* in Victorian moralism, Herderian romanticism, and the historical realism of the gospels (sorrow songs). Zamir suggests that Du Bois's sense of the tragic goes a bit deeper than I admit—but only a little bit deeper. See Shamoon Zamir, "'The Sorrow Songs'/ 'Song of Myself': Du Bois, The Crisis of Leadership, and Prophetic Imagination," in *The Black Columbiad: Defining Moments in African American Literature and Culture,* ed. Werner Sollors and Maria Diedrich (Cambridge: Harvard University Press, 1994), pp. 145–66, esp. 147–48. For Zamir's fascinating, yet ultimately unconvincing Hegelian treatment of Du Bois's early thought, see *Dark Voices: W. E. B. Du Bois and American Thought, 1888–1903* (Chicago: University of Chicago Press, 1995). For Du Bois on jazz, see Kathy J. Ogren, *The Jazz Revolution: Twenties America and the Meaning of Jazz* (New York: Oxford University Press, 1989), pp. 118–20.

7. For a provocative recent treatment of this age-old dichotomy created by intellectuals—the ultimate logic of which denies the full human status of the majority of people—see John Carey, *The Intellectuals and the Masses: Pride and Prejudice Among the Literary Intelligentsia, 1880–1939* (New York: St. Martin's Press, 1992). For direct references to black people—some of which resonate with Du Bois's—note pp. 52, 65, 121, 125, 148, 194f., 210. Needless to say, most of the figures Carey examines—such as José Ortega y Gasset, Knut Hamsun, T. S. Eliot, H. G. Wells, W. B. Yeats, Evelyn Waugh, Arthur Machen, George Bernard Shaw, Ezra Pound, Wyndham Lewis, D. H. Lawrence, and Aldous Huxley—were either arch elitists or outright xenophobes. Du Bois's democratic sentiments tempered his elitism and xenophobia (e.g., his anti-Jewish stereotypes were toned down in later editions of *The Souls of Black Folk*). For example, note David Levering Lewis's analysis in *W. E. B. Du Bois,* p. 285.

8. Du Bois, *Dusk of Dawn*, in *Writings,* p. 596.

9. W. E. B. Du Bois, *The Autobiography of W. E. B. Du Bois: A Soliloquy on Viewing My Life from the Last Decade of Its First Century* (New York: International Publishers, 1968), pp. 221–22.

10. Lewis, *W. E. B. Du Bois,* p. 227.

11. This brief tilt toward the tragic in Du Bois's corpus may be contrasted with that most rare of despairing moments in Ralph Waldo Emerson's upbeat writings—namely, his often overlooked poem "Threnody," one of the great elegies in the English language, written in response to the death of his beloved five-year-old first son, Waldo. Note how Emerson wrestles with the overwhelming *irrevocability* of his son's death in its opening lines, with no reaching for reason or revelation:

> The South-wind brings
> Life, sunshine and desire,
> And on every mount and meadow
> Breathes aromatic fire;
> But over the dead he has no power,
> The lost, the lost, he cannot restore;
> And, looking over the hills, I mourn
> The darling who shall not return.

12. Du Bois, *The Souls of Black Folk,* pp. 154–55. See also Keith E. Byerman, *Seizing the Word: History, Art, and Self in the Work of W. E. B. Du Bois* (Athens: University of Georgia Press, 1994), pp. 29–31.

13. Du Bois, *The Souls of Black Folk,* p. 153.

14. For a fascinating yet unpersuasive reading of this neglected moment in Du Bois which claims that "this suffering has no redemptive moment," see Paul Gilroy, *The Black Atlantic: Modernity and Double Consciousness* (Cambridge: Harvard University Press, 1993), pp. 138–39. Gilroy rightly points out that Du Bois experiences "an awful gladness in my heart. . . . No bitter meanness now shall sicken his baby heart till it die a living death, no taunt shall madden his happy boyhood. Fool that I was to think or wish that this little soul should grow choked and deformed within the Veil! . . . Better far this nameless void that stops

my life than a sea of sorrows for you" (Du Bois, *The Souls of Black Folk*, p. 156). Yet the first sentence of the chapter—"Unto you a child is born"—invokes Jesus of Nazareth (that most redemptive of figures). Du Bois also hears "in his baby voice the voice of the Prophet that was to rise within the Veil" while his son is alive. And he vows that his son's death "is not the end. Surely there shall yet dawn some mighty morning to lift the Veil and set the prisoned free. Not for me,—I shall die in my bonds,—but for fresh young souls who have not known the night and waken to the morning . . . some morning. . . ." (p. 156). This certainly is Du Bois in a tragic mood, yet his Enlightenment eschatology—with a small dose of Stoicism—gets the best of him. Like Candide in that marvelous Enlightenment novelette *Candide* (1759) by the inimitable Voltaire, even in the midst of the deepest tragedies and absurdities, cultivation can still generate a harvest, rational control and moral action can still yield fruit down the road. In fact, Du Bois's salvific sentiments provide more hope for the future than Voltaire's witty and resilient Stoicism. Only Du Bois's incredible and torturous prayer in response to the Atlanta Riot—his classic "A Litany of Atlanta" (1906)—explores the tragic and absurd depths of the human condition. His desperate call for moral integrity and political action in the face of the "white terror" of human suffering and divine silence, as well as his embrace of the "dark sleep," is one instance in his corpus where he engages in the existential deep-sea diving of Tolstoy, Chekhov, Kafka, Coltrane, and Morrison. For this sterling performance, see James Melvin Washington's canonical text, *Conversations with God: Two Centuries of Prayers by African Americans* (New York: HarperCollins, 1994), pp. 102-4. Washington's profound "Afterword: A Scholar's Benediction" captures my own Christian tragicomic sense of life—a sense grounded in the Christocentric humanism of Erasmus, Kierkegaard, and Martin Luther King, Jr.; the tormented love ethic of Tennessee Williams, Leo Tolstoy, and Toni Morrison; and the indefatigable compassion of Anton Chekhov, Muriel Rukeyser, and John Coltrane. My own perennial wrestling with existential tension in history is deeply influenced by the profound corpus of Eric Voegelin.

15. For Du Bois's direct debt to the father of Victorian social criticism, Thomas Carlyle, see Lewis, *W. E. B. Du Bois,* pp. 74–75, 77, 78, 115–16, 120, 136, 148. The best general treatment of Carlyle's life and work is Fred Kaplan's *Thomas Carlyle: A Biography* (Berkeley: University of California Press, 1983).

16. Du Bois, "The Talented Tenth," in *Writings,* pp. 842, 861.

17. Du Bois's critique of patriarchy—black and white—grows and deepens in the course of his long career. For instance, see his 1920 classic essay, "The Damnation of Women," from *Darkwater,* in *Writings,* pp. 952–68.

18. Matthew Arnold, *Culture and Anarchy,* ed. J. Dover Wilson (Cambridge: Cambridge University Press, 1960), p. 70.

19. Du Bois, "The Talented Tenth," in *Writings,* pp. 846, 847.

20. For superb synoptic treatments of two exemplary figures, see Thomas C. Holt, "The Lonely Warrior: Ida B. Wells-Barnett and the Struggle for Black Leadership," in *Black Leaders of the Twentieth Century,* ed. John Hope Franklin and August Meier (Urbana: University of Illinois Press, 1982), pp. 39–61; and Joseph P. Reidy, "Aaron A. Bradley: The Voice of Black Labor in the Georgia Lowcountry," in *Southern Black Leaders of the Reconstruction Era,* ed. Howard N. Rabinowitz (Urbana: University of Illinois Press, 1982), pp. 281–308.

21. Du Bois acknowledges this fact in *Dusk of Dawn* (in *Writings,* p. 690): "It still remains possible in the United States for a white American to be a gentleman and a scholar, a Christian and a man of integrity, and yet flatly and openly refuse to treat as a fellow human being any person who has Negro ancestry." As in Leo Tolstoy's magnificent short story "After the Ball" (1903), in which a genteel old colonel masks his hatred and cruelty toward a lower-class person, this paradox and hypocrisy undermines one of the crucial "truths" of the Enlightenment worldview and Victorian social criticism.

22. W. E. B. Du Bois, "The Talented Tenth: Memorial Address" (1948), in *A Reader,* ed. David Levering Lewis (New York: Henry Holt & Co., 1995), p. 349.

23. Ibid., p. 350.

24. Two neglected gems in the rich Victorian tradition of so-

cial criticism especially pertinent in our precatastrophic postmodern times are L. T. Hobhouse, *Democracy and Reaction* (1904) and C. F. G. Masterman, *The Condition of England* (1909). In the former text, Hobhouse—a great anti-imperialist democrat of Edwardian England—echoes Du Bois's famous claim that "the problem of the twentieth century is the problem of the color-line." In the latter book, Masterman—the sagacious critic of English self-deception just prior to World War I—writes,

> Humanity—at best—appears but as a shipwrecked crew which has taken refuge on a narrow ledge of rock, beaten by wind and wave; which cannot tell how many, if any at all, will survive when the long night gives place to morning. The wise man will still go softly all his days; working always for greater economic equality on the one hand, for understanding between estranged peoples on the other; apprehending always how slight an effort of stupidity or violence could strike a death blow to twentieth-century civilization, and elevate the forces of destruction triumphant over the ruins of a world. (London: Methuen & Co., 1909; p. 233)

25. George Steiner, "A Responsion," in *Reading George Steiner,* ed. Nathan A. Scott, Jr., and Ronald A. Sharp (Baltimore: Johns Hopkins University Press, 1994), p. 278. Steiner's critical attitude toward the academy echoes that of the grand old (Canadian-born) Harvard humanist Douglas Bush. His 1966 book on the greatest nineteenth-century English poet, John Keats, is one of the best we have, and his 1939 Alexander Lectures lament the loss of the "general reader." In the latter he states,

> One may wonder, timidly, if a real revival of the humanities might not be inaugurated by a moratorium on productive scholarship . . . long enough to restore our perspective and sense of value. What a golden interlude we might have, with the learned journals temporarily withdrawn, with no scholarly lucubrations to read or write, no annual bibliographies to torment us with hundreds of things we must know if we are to be qualified to lead hopeful young men into the same

labyrinth, with nothing to do, in short, but sit down in peace with the great books we ought to be soaking in! . . . In front of my desk are serried rows of card-indexes, bibliographies, and periodicals. Out of sight behind me are Holbein's portraits of Erasmus and More. "Saint Socrates, pray for us." (Quoted from Douglas Bush, *The Renaissance and English Humanism* [Toronto: University of Toronto Press, 1939], pp. 132–33)

For one of the most powerful critiques of professionalized cultural studies in this century, see Geoffrey Scott's classic *The Architecture of Humanism: A Study in the History of Taste* (1914; reprint, New York: W. W. Norton & Co., 1974).

26. For a brief examination of the slow demise of American exceptionalism in American historiography, see David W. Noble, *The End of American History* (Minneapolis: University of Minnesota, 1985). Note also Michael Kammen, "The Problem of American Exceptionalism: A Reconsideration," *American Quarterly* 45, no. 1 (1993): pp. 1–43.

27. Du Bois confronts this pessimism most strikingly in two of the most insightful and angry essays in his corpus—"The White World," in *Dusk of Dawn* (1940), and "The Souls of White Folk," in *Darkwater* (1920). These essays echo the themes in the work of the grand dean of Pan-African Studies in America, John Henrik Clarke. But in neither essay does Du Bois openly acknowledge that a long tradition of black cultural and revolutionary nationalists had already arrived where he seemed to be headed. Harold Cruse makes this persuasive argument in his classic work, *The Crisis of the Negro Intellectual* (New York: William Morrow & Co., 1967), pp. 330–36. For Du Bois's essays, see *Writings,* pp. 652–80, 923–38.

28. Henry Highland Garnet, "An Address to the Slaves of the United States of America of 1843," in *Black Nationalism in America,* ed. John Bracey, August Meier, and Elliot Rudwick (Indianapolis: Bobbs-Merrill, 1970), p. 73.

29. It is no accident that these two groups serve as major preoccupations of the two towering European men of letters in our

time—Isaiah Berlin and George Steiner. The recent revival around Berlin focuses on his pluralistic liberal political thought, but his greatness resides in his deep and empathetic interpretations of Russian intellectuals such as Turgenev, Belinsky, Bakunin, and especially Herzen and Tolstoy. His powerful readings of Vico, Herder, and de Maistre—though canonical—pale in the face of his self-invested and magisterial treatments of Tolstoy. In fact, his most famous essay, "The Hedgehog and the Fox" (originally entitled, in its shorter form, "Lev Tolstoy's Historical Scepticism"), is the best example of philosophic *phronesis* (practical wisdom) in this blood-drenched century. Section 6 of this magnificent essay—the pinnacle of his masterful corpus—represents the highest form of philosophic literature written in twentieth-century Europe—and Tolstoy is his major springboard. This essay, to be read and reread, is found in *Russian Thinkers,* ed. Henry Hardy and Aileen Kelly (New York: Viking Press, 1978), pp. 22–81, esp. 68–74. George Steiner's gallant attempt to focus our attention on early twentieth-century Central European figures such as Hermann Broch, Paul Celan, Arnold Schoenberg, Robert Musil, Sigmund Freud, Rainer Maria Rilke, and Franz Kafka is monumental and has yielded much fruit. For example, recent interest in Musil—due in part to the new edition of his novel *The Man Without Qualities* (1930), including previously unpublished sections, and of his timely essays, *Precision and Soul* (Chicago: University of Chicago Press, 1990), ed. Burton Pike and David S. Luft—is growing. A Broch revival centered on his masterpiece, *The Death of Virgil* (1945), may be next. Yet Steiner's project began with the Russians—that is, with Tolstoy, Dostoyevsky, and Shestov. His first book was *Tolstoy or Dostoevsky: An Essay in the Old Criticism* (New York: Knopf, 1959)—Tolstoy as Homeric bard vs. Dostoyevsky as tragic dramatist in response to the "dilemma of Realism" created by Dickens, Hugo, Stendhal, Zola, and Flaubert. And the great work of Shestov (whose first book was on Shakespeare), *Athens and Jerusalem,* deeply influenced him. Steiner notes, "The nearing shadow of Hitler made me. . . . [T]he dialectic of 'Athens/Jerusalem' has been perennial throughout my teaching and published work." And notwithstanding his marvelous readings of Kafka—a figure who shunned noise and music—Steiner states, "The question 'what in the world is music like?' has become for me the metaphysical inquiry incarnate. . . . [I]t is, in Levi-Strauss's arresting formulation, the invention of melody which remains the *mystère suprême des sciences de l'homme.*" See Steiner, "A Responsion," in *Reading George Steiner,* pp. 276, 280, 283, 284. Note the brilliant essays pertinent to my concerns in this superb volume by Robert Boyers, Guido Almansi, Ruth Padel, Edith Wyschogrod, John Bayley, and especially Caryl Emerson. For a seminal effort to connect black arts to nineteenth-century Russian literature—in a call for "universalized particularity"—see Alain Locke, "Self-Criticism: The Third Dimension in Culture," *Phylon* 11 (1950): pp. 391–94. My attempt to link the situation in *fin-de-siècle* Russia, early twentieth-century Central Europe, and late twentieth-century black America rests in part on possible connections between Tolstoy, Kafka, and black artists like John Coltrane and Toni Morrison. For a brief contrast of Tolstoy and Kafka, see Pietro Citati, *Tolstoy* (New York: Schocken Books, 1986), pp. 223–25. For fascinating and suggestive connections between Tolstoy, Chekhov, and jazz, note Nabokov's pregnant remarks about the distinctive genius of Tolstoy—his "time-balance"; "his characters seem to move with the same swing as the people passing under our window"; "Tolstoy's prose keeps pace with our pulses"; or "the perfectly natural swing" in Chekhov's *The Seagull.* This characterization resonates with the formal improvisational freedom, "metrical adventurousness," verbal playfulness, and syncopated responsiveness associated with black cultural expression—especially its most sophisticated artistic works, such as those of John Coltrane and Toni Morrison. Note Vladimir Nabokov, *Lectures on Russian Literature,* ed. Fredson Bowers (New York: Harcourt Brace & Co., 1981), pp. 141–42, 282. An important historical treatment of the evolution of black culture is Roger D. Abrahams's *Singing the Master: The Emergence of African-American Culture in the Plantation South* (New York: Penguin Books, 1992). The best recent synoptic treatment of the origins of black culture is Sterling Stuckey's *Slave Culture: Nationalist Theory and the Foundations of Black America* (New York: Oxford University Press, 1987). A more interpretive examination of black music is Leroi Jones's classic, *Blues People* (New York: William Morrow & Co., 1963). The complex relation of the world-historical efforts of Tolstoy and Kafka to those of Armstrong, Ellington, Coltrane, and Morrison to transfigure sadness and sorrow into great art based on meticulous explorations of the quotidian realities of degraded and devalued peoples requires serious inquiry in the future. How do we account for these three incredible artistic peaks—Russian novelistic and theatrical preeminence, Central European literary and epistolary achievements, and twentieth-century black musical and literary supremacy—in late modernity?

30. Du Bois's debt to Goethe's *Faust* was profound. And the word "striving" was—along with "enjoyment"—the most Faustian of terms, rooted in Goethe's own idiosyncratic theory of entelechy in nature and man. "Striving" consists of a fundamental human urge to embrace the world and takes the form of self-expression in thought and, above all, action. The famous last words of Faust in Goethe's incomparable modern epic poem are worth quoting here—they get at the heart and core of Du Bois's worldview:

> Yes—this I hold to with devout insistence,
> Wisdom's last verdict goes to say:
> He only earns both freedom and existence
> Who must reconquer them each day.
> And so, ringed all about by perils, here
> Youth, manhood, age will spend their strenuous year.
> Such teeming would I see upon this land,
> On acres free among free people stand.
> I might entreat the fleeting minute:
> Oh tarry yet, thou art so fair!
> My path on earth, the trace I leave within it
> Eons untold cannot impair.
> Foretasting such high happiness to come,
> I savor now my striving's crown and sum.

For Du Bois's special love for Goethe's work and his advice to Fisk University students and graduates to immerse themselves in Goethe in order to expedite "the rise of the Negro people," see Lewis, *W. E. B. Du Bois,* p. 139. For a comprehensive and incisive reading of Du Bois's *The Souls of Black Folk* as itself a "striving" in the form of a textual performance and narrative experiment in dramatic form, see Sundquist, *To Wake the Nations,* pp. 457–539.

31. Du Bois, *The Souls of Black Folk,* p. 15. Du Bois's allusion to a European poet's powerful metaphor of crying seems to echo the opening of Anna Julia Cooper's classic *A Voice from the South* (1892)—the first major work of a black woman of letters in the U.S., which inspired the powerful writings of black women intellectuals like bell hooks, Patricia Williams, Deborah McDowell, Kimberle Crenshaw, Alice Walker, Katie Cannon, Hazel Carby, Michele Wallace, Paula Giddings, Wahneema Lubiano, Hortense Spillers, Angela Davis, Tricia Rose, Valerie Smith, and Farah Griffin in our day. In the preface, Cooper begins,

> In the clash and clatter of our American Conflict, it has been said that the South remains Silent. Like the Sphinx she inspires vociferous disputation, but herself takes little part in the noisy controversy. One muffled strain in the Silent South, a jarring chord and a vague and uncomprehended cadenza, has been and still is the Negro. And of that muffled chord, the one mute and voiceless note has been the sadly expectant Black woman,

> > An infant crying in the night,
> > An infant crying for the light.
> > And with *no language—but a cry.*

Cooper's explicit allusion to the self-description of nineteenth-century Europe's great lyrical poet Alfred Tennyson—with his themes of the terror of loneliness and the preoccupation with death—resonates with the beginning of Du Bois's text. W. H. Auden's famous characterization of Tennyson seems to apply to the existential starting points of both Cooper and Du Bois:

Two questions: Who am I? Why do I exist? and the panic fear of their remaining unanswered—doubt is much too intellectual and tame a term for such a vertigo of anxiety— seem to have obsessed him all his life. . . .

Tennyson became conscious in childhood of Hamlet's problem, the religious significance of his own experience.

In short, the black predicament first emerged as Hamlet's problem—the radical contingency of life, the sheer indifference of nature, and human destructive thought and self-destructive action. Like the Russian intellectuals' obsession with Hamlet—from Turgenev's torment in his influential essay on Hamlet (and Don Quixote) in 1860 to Tolstoy's scorn in his infamous renunciation of Shakespeare in 1906 and Kafka's appreciation of Shakespeare (thanks to his Anglophilic friend Emil Weiss), despite his disorientating experience of seeing Albert Bassermann perform Hamlet in Berlin in 1910—the tragedies and absurdities bombarding black people in the New World made Hamlet's problem even more intense and urgent. In Tennyson's case, this intensity and urgency was due in part to an unhappy childhood at home and school (Louth Grammar School) and the early death of his best friend, Arthur Henry Hallam. For the quote in Anna Julia Cooper, see *A Voice from the South,* introduction by Mary Helen Washington, Schomburg Library of Nineteenth-Century Black Women Writers, Henry Louis Gates, Jr., gen. ed. (New York: Oxford University Press, 1988), p. i. For W. H. Auden's quotes, see "Tennyson," in *Forewords and Afterwords* (New York: Vintage Books, 1989), pp. 228, 229. For Kafka's brush with Shakespeare, see Ernst Pawel, *The Nightmare of Reason: A Life of Franz Kafka* (New York: Vintage Books, 1984), pp. 127, 217; and Frederick Karl, *Franz Kafka: Representative Man* (New York: Fromm International, 1991), pp. 252, 259. Hamlet's famous lines "The time is out of joint—O cursed spite, / That ever I was born to set it right!" and "To be, or not to be, that is the question" are fundamental themes in black strivings. This is why *flight* and *flow*— migration and emigration, experimentation and improvisation—are so basic to black history and life. And also why Hamlet's motifs of *mourning* and *revenge* are two dominant elements in the black cultural and political unconscious.

32. Du Bois, *The Souls of Black Folk*, p. 15.

33. Ibid.

34. This vicious white supremacist reduction makes it difficult for black people to discuss and display their full humanity and variety among themselves—most clearly seen in the underdeveloped discourse on black sexuality in our era of AIDS. The formidable example of black gay intellectuals like the late Marlon Riggs and Kendall Thomas and black lesbian intellectuals such as the late Audre Lorde and Barbara Smith is indispensable in resisting this inhumane reduction.

35. Ralph Ellison, *Invisible Man* (New York: New American Library, 1952), p. 7.

36. Du Bois, *The Souls of Black Folk*, p. 148.

37. Ibid., p. 149.

38. Ibid., p. 150.

39. Ibid.

40. Ibid., pp. 16–17.

41. Toni Morrison, *Beloved* (New York: New American Library, 1987), p. 140.

42. Ibid., p. 251.

43. Ibid.

44. Du Bois, *The Souls of Black Folk*, p. 156.

45. James Baldwin, *Go Tell It on the Mountain* (New York: Dell Publishing Co., 1953), pp. 137–38.

46. Like Nina's precious words at the end of Chekhov's *The Seagull*, "Know how to bear your cross and have faith," or Irina's at the conclusion of *The Three Sisters*, "I'll give my whole life to those who may need it."

47. Morrison, *Beloved*, pp. 87, 88–89.

48. Du Bois, *The Souls of Black Folk*, p. 157.

49. Ibid., p. 158.

50. Richard Wright, *Native Son* (New York: Harper & Row, 1940), pp. 20–21.

51. Ibid., pp. 285–86.

52. Ibid., p. 275.

53. Ibid., p. 277. Note Wright's allusion to "the last best hope of earth"—"America"—in Lincoln's famous message to Congress on December 1, 1862: "We shall nobly save, or meanly lose, the last best hope of earth." See Mark E. Neely, Jr., *The Last Best Hope of Earth: Abraham Lincoln and the Promise of America* (Cambridge: Harvard University Press, 1993), p. v.

54. Wright, *Native Son*, p. 268.

55. Du Bois, *The Souls of Black Folk*, p. 159.

56. Needless to say, this theme of bondage applies above all to those obsessed not simply with oppression but with the sheer concrete fact and potency of evil. Bigger's existential nihilism—his inability to run from himself (including the white supremacy in him)—echoes that of Ahab in Melville's classic *Moby-Dick* (1851), Attwater in Robert Louis Stevenson's late masterpiece, *The Ebb-Tide* (1894), and Kurtz in Joseph Conrad's famous *Heart of Darkness* (1902).

57. Wright, *Native Son*, pp. 22–23.

58. Ibid., p. 388.

59. Du Bois, *The Souls of Black Folk*, p. 146.

60. Wright, *Native Son*, pp. 237, 238.

61. Ellison, *Invisible Man*, p. 11. For a fuller and richer elaboration of this Ellisonian insight, the classic works of Albert Murray, *Stomping the Blues* and *The Hero and the Blues*, are peerless.

62. Du Bois, *The Souls of Black Folk*, p. 161.

63. Wright, *Native Son*, pp. 109–10.

64. Du Bois, *The Souls of Black Folk*, p. 164.

65. Ibid.

66. Ibid., pp. 164–65.

67. Ibid., pp. 23, 41.

68. Richard J. Barnet and John Cavanagh, *Global Dreams: Imperial Corporations and the New World Order* (New York: Simon & Schuster, 1994). See also Benjamin R. Barber, *Jihad vs. McWorld* (New York: Random House, 1995).

69. For a powerful treatment of the negative impact of globalization on the most disadvantaged and vulnerable human beings on the globe, see Herb Addo (the major exponent of neoradical creative pessimism), "The Convulsive Historical Mo-

ment: Considerations from a Neoradical Third World Perspective," *Macalaster International* 1 (Spring 1995): pp. 115–48. Addo's sophisticated Neo-Marxism leads him to conclude: "1) History is not just any old absurdity, but a patently silly absurdity; 2) global life is not only just a drama, but a dark drama; and 3) the Third World role in both is not just any old invigorating happy laughing farce, but a huge bad-humored farce" (p. 115). This apocalyptic—yet far from outlandish—prospect is also entertained in Giovanni Arrighi's magisterial *The Long Twentieth Century: Money, Power, and the Origins of Our Old Times* (New York: Verso, 1994), in which he concludes that humanity "may well burn up in the horrors (or glories) of the escalating violence that has accompanied the liquidation of the Cold War world order. In this case, capitalist history would also come to an end but by reverting permanently to the systemic chaos from which it began six hundred years ago and which has been reproduced on an ever-increasing scale with each transition. Whether this would mean the end just of capitalist history or of all human history, it is impossible to tell" (p. 356). Eric Hobsbawm reaches similar conclusions—but with a small dose of English reticence: "Our world risks both explosion and implosion. It must change. . . . If humanity is to have a recognizable future, it cannot be by prolonging the past or the present. If we try to build the third millennium on that basis, we shall fail. And the price of failure, that is to say, the alternative to a changed society, is darkness" (Hobsbawm, *The Age of Extremes,* p. 585). The most recent erudite world historian to look into the future and risk the curse of Cassandra is Felipe Fernandez-Armesto, who claims that "the day of democracy looks as if it has arrived, but it will prove to be a false dawn or a short spell of wintry light. . . . [R]ecrudescent fascism is the great political menace of the near future. . . . Ethnic enmity is likely to continue to be a breaker of states. . . . [I]t seems inevitable that in the next century the world will experience more rounds of ethnic cleansing . . . the massacres will be bloodier and the conflicts more prolonged. . . . [T]he world, I feel tempted to conclude, will go on getting worse." *Millennium: A History of the Last Thousand Years* (New York: Scribner, 1995), pp. 726, 727,

732, 736. Thomas M. Callaghy and John Ravenhill desperately attempt to temper such pessimism in "Vision, Politics, and Structure: Afro-Optimism, Afro-Pessimism or Realism?" and "How Hemmed In? Lessons and Prospects of Africa's Responses to Decline," in *Hemmed In: Responses to Africa's Economic Decline*, ed. Thomas M. Callaghy and John Ravenhill (New York: Columbia University Press, 1993), pp. 1–17, 520–63.

70. For the incredible empirical figures revealing the disparity between the wealthy and others, see Edward N. Wolff, *Top Heavy: A Study of the Increasing Inequality of Wealth in America* (New York: Twentieth Century Fund Press, 1995), pp. 7, 10, 11. For the two most important books on the decay of American democracy concealed by the political rule of liberal and especially right-wing elites, see the work of the progressive populist William Greider, *Who Will Tell the People?: The Betrayal of American Democracy* (New York: Simon & Schuster, 1992); and that of the conservative populist Kevin Phillips, *Boiling Point: Republicans, Democrats, and the Decline of Middle-Class Prosperity* (New York: Random House, 1993).

71. Quoted from Gerald Horne, *Black and Red: W. E. B. Du Bois and the Afro-American Response to the Cold War* (Albany: State University of New York Press, 1986), p. 345.

72. A. N. Wilson, *Tolstoy* (New York: Fawcett Columbine, 1988), p. 257.

73. Pawel, *The Nightmare of Reason*, pp. 368, 427–30. Kafka writes, "I realized that if I somehow wanted to go on living, I had to do something quite radical, and so I decided to emigrate to Palestine. I probably would not have been able to do so; I am also quite unprepared in Hebrew and in other respects, but I simply had to have hope of some kind to latch on to." Although Kafka was not a Zionist, he might well have emigrated to Palestine if tuberculosis of the larynx had not ended his short life. Like John Coltrane, Franz Kafka died at forty.